C.R.A.F.T.

CONVERSATIONS
FOR TEACHER GROWTH

C.R.A.F.T.

CONVERSATIONS
FOR TEACHER GROWTH

How to Build Bridges and Cultivate Expertise

SALLY J.
ZEPEDA

LAKESHA ROBINSON
GOFF

STEFANIE W.
STEELE

Alexandria, Virginia USA

1703 N. Beauregard St. • Alexandria, VA 22311-1714 USA
Phone: 800-933-2723 or 703-578-9600 • Fax: 703-575-5400
Website: www.ascd.org • E-mail: member@ascd.org
Author guidelines: www.ascd.org/write

Ronn Nozoe, *Interim CEO & Executive Director;* Stefani Roth, *Publisher;* Genny Ostertag, *Director, Content Acquisitions;* Susan Hills, *Acquisitions Editor;* Julie Houtz, *Director, Book Editing & Production;* Miriam Calderone, *Editor;* Judi Connelly, *Senior Art Director;* Melissa Johnston, *Graphic Designer;* Cynthia Stock, *Typesetter;* Kelly Marshall, *Interim Manager, Production Services;* Trinay Blake, *E-Publishing Specialist*

All web links in this book are correct as of the publication date below but may have become inactive or otherwise modified since that time. If you notice a deactivated or changed link, please e-mail books@ascd.org with the words "Link Update" in the subject line. In your message, please specify the web link, the book title, and the page number on which the link appears.

PAPERBACK ISBN: 978-1-4166-2805-7   ASCD product #120001   n8/19
PDF E-BOOK ISBN: 978-1-4166-2807-1; see Books in Print for other formats.

Quantity discounts are available: e-mail programteam@ascd.org or call 800-933-2723, ext. 5773, or 703-575-5773. For desk copies, go to www.ascd.org/deskcopy.

Library of Congress Cataloging-in-Publication Data is available for this title.
Library of Congress Control Number:2019021037

----

27 26 25 24 23 22 21 20 19   1 2 3 4 5 6 7 8 9 10 11 12

C.R.A.F.T.

CONVERSATIONS
FOR TEACHER GROWTH

How to Build Bridges and Cultivate Expertise

Acknowledgments

We are appreciative of the support and encouragement of Susan Hills, acquisitions editor for ASCD. Susan was thorough and offered wise counsel and encouragement along the way, making writing this book an adventure in what's possible. Book editor Miriam Calderone was instrumental in shepherding our manuscript through all editorial processes to get to the finish line. Graphic designer Melissa Johnston spent considerable time getting the cover design "just right." We also appreciate the feedback from external reviewers and the countless professionals at ASCD who brought this book into print. Critical friends—Phyllis Owen, Theresa Braddy, Kathy Hodges, and Tina Smosny—were gracious in providing feedback on the C.R.A.F.T. Conversation Café Protocol.

Introduction

One of the best ways for administrators to have a lasting positive impact on their schools is to foster effective, ongoing relationship-building and communication skills. The impact of these skills—or the lack of them—is impressive: research has shown that the main reason new teachers leave the profession is not workload, administrative duties, unavailability of resources, or lack of professional development opportunities but, rather, relationships with school leadership (Burkhauser, 2017; Kraft, Marinell, & Shen-Wei Yee, 2016).

What can administrators do to improve these relationships? They must improve their conversations—and helping them to do so is precisely the goal of this book. In the chapters that follow, we will show you how what we call "C.R.A.F.T. conversations" can make a positive difference for professional relationships and practice, and we will outline the skills and processes that will help you adapt and use this powerful approach in your own work.

Part I of this book comprises two chapters that establish the foundation for C.R.A.F.T. conversations. Chapter 1 makes the case for the urgent need for school personnel to engage in conversations that matter and describes how these types of conversations lead to nurturing the growth and development of teachers and administrators. We promote the notion that conversation craftsmanship is a people-centered, multidimensional skill set that necessitates both a mindset that values face-to-face discussion and an unconditional willingness to commit to intentional and purposeful planning, reflection, and follow-up. In Chapter 1 we also explore the acronym *C.R.A.F.T.* to describe the kinds of conversations—*c*lear, *r*ealistic, *a*ppropriate, *f*lexible, and *t*imely—that help educators grow their practice. We then introduce the four cornerstones of C.R.A.F.T. conversations: Building Capacity, Invoking Change, Promoting Collaboration, and Prioritizing Celebration. In Chapter 2 we extend the discussion of the four cornerstones, illustrating the embedded nature of each one and showing how they come together to build a strong, lasting foundation that can lead to positive and sustainable change.

In Part II, we build from the foundation to show you what C.R.A.F.T. conversations look like in implementation. Chapters 3 through 5 unpack the first four components of C.R.A.F.T. conversations: planning, opening, engaging, and closing. Together, these four elements lead to conversations that place teachers and leaders directly on the road to success. Chapter 6 focuses on the last two components of C.R.A.F.T. conversations, which are often overlooked: reflecting and following up. Because these two essential steps will ultimately make or break a conversation, we discuss common challenges and offer strategies for both. In Chapter 7, we discuss final takeaways to support leaders and teachers in their efforts to engage in C.R.A.F.T. conversations.

In describing each of the components, we include actions you can take that relate to the five elements of the acronym *C.R.A.F.T.* (*c*lear, *r*ealistic, *a*ppropriate, *f*lexible, and *t*imely). We also refer to the four cornerstones to ensure that each conversation has the potential to build capacity, invoke change, promote collaboration, and prioritize celebration.

Throughout the book, you'll find not only advice and examples (including sample conversations between administrators and teachers, and reflective questions related to each cornerstone) but also tools that will help you put the ideas into practice right away. It is our hope that this book will help you harness the power of great conversations to build capacity across your school, deepen your professional relationships, and make a positive difference in outcomes for kids. Let's get started!

PART I

Laying the Foundation for C.R.A.F.T. Conversations

1 The C.R.A.F.T. Conversation Difference

Be brave enough to start a conversation that matters.

—Margaret Wheatley, *Turning to One Another* (2002)

INSIDE THIS CHAPTER:

- What Is a C.R.A.F.T. Conversation?
- The Four Cornerstones of C.R.A.F.T. Conversations
- Key Components of a C.R.A.F.T. Conversation

Craft—an activity requiring skill; skill in carrying out one's work

Conversation—a skillful formal or informal oral exchange to explore perspectives and ideas, uncover misconceptions, and collaboratively problem-solve

C.R.A.F.T. Conversation—a skillful formal or informal oral exchange to explore perspectives and ideas, uncover misconceptions, and collaboratively problem-solve in a *c*lear, *r*ealistic, *a*ppropriate, *f*lexible, and *t*imely fashion; a conversation that does one or more of the following: builds capacity, invokes change, promotes collaboration, prioritizes celebration

Monica recently transferred to a new school as an assistant principal, and her main responsibility is defined as "improving teacher quality." At the orientation for new teachers, Monica makes it a priority to meet and converse with as many new teachers as possible. During lunch, she does not follow the other administrators, who retreat to the back of the cafeteria to sit as a group. Instead, Monica invites herself to sit with a small group of first-year teachers.

Through conversation, Monica finds out that one of the new teachers, Jennifer, is part of an alternative certification program. Jennifer talks about the preparation courses that she has completed so far and highlights a recent assignment—creating a detailed script for the first day of school—that is proving to be more difficult than she had anticipated.

Monica immediately thinks about some valuable resources she has gathered over the years that would be helpful as Jennifer begins her assignment. She knows that this is an opportunity to begin the work of establishing a strong and trusting relationship with one of her new teachers. When she offers to meet with Jennifer later that same day, Jennifer enthusiastically agrees. As Monica finishes her lunch, she mentally reviews the key components of a C.R.A.F.T. conversation to set herself up for success.

Conversations. How often do you stop and think about them? Can you recall conversations you have had with colleagues, some that were thought-provoking and engaging and others you simply wish you could forget? Can you visualize that one person who always seems to know the right thing to say, at just the right moment, and in just the right place? Meaningful conversations may come naturally to some, but for many people, it takes skill and thoughtful planning to frame conversations that count.

With everything that lies on the educational landscape today, from personalized online learning to professional learning communities

(PLCs), there is no question that high-quality conversations are integral to school improvement and success. If you were to ask most school leaders about conversations in their school, they would probably say that conversations occur frequently and across every imaginable setting, from the front office to the bus lane. However, the real question leaders should be asking is this: how many of these conversations really count?

You might be wondering what exactly makes a conversation count. It would be awesome if we could provide you with a checklist of specific criteria, but that's simply not the nature of conversations. To determine whether or not a conversation counts, you must refer back to its intended purpose. What were you trying to achieve? The answer to this question will vary. The one constant is that when it comes to making conversations count, it all begins and ends with people.

The quality of a conversation centers around the people involved. Key conversations that literally changed history are prime examples that show us that some people are just not skilled at crafting successful conversations, whereas others could be deemed naturals. Think about the "smoking gun" conversations that ultimately led to the resignation of President Richard Nixon. He probably had no idea his taped Watergate conversations would lead to his political demise.

By contrast, think about President John F. Kennedy. He was definitely a natural when it came to effective conversations. Following the Soviet Union's launch of Sputnik in 1957, he initiated the "Race to the Moon" in 1961, proclaiming that the United States would be the first nation to put a man on the moon by the end of the decade. Many of his captivating speeches that followed were based on quality conversations he had had with other world leaders. Eight years later, in July of 1969, the Apollo 11 moon-walk mission took place. Imagine the types of conversations that had to occur to make his dream become a reality for the nation!

In the present age of digital communication, championed by such iconic figures as Steve Jobs and Mark Zuckerberg, the nature of conversation has changed significantly. We find ourselves enthralled with abbreviated conversation in various forms: on-screen through e-mail, 280 characters in a tweet, a few hashtags on Instagram, or a Facebook post. Do these conversations *count*? Millennials and social media fans alike would say yes! However, when we consider today's schools, conversations that count must go deeper. They require a skill set that is people-centered, a mindset that values face-to-face discussion, and a willingness to commit to intentional and purposeful planning, reflection, and follow-up. In other words, conversations that count take quite a bit of craftsmanship.

The word *craftsmanship* might seem like an odd choice until you take a moment to think about the uncanny power of conversations. They can energize or deflate. They can empower or devalue. They can inspire or create dissension. Every conversation has an infinite amount of potential, and because of that, there is an art to maximizing the moment. As authors, we collectively have more than 80 years of experience working with teachers and school leaders, and if there's one thing we agree upon, it's that conversations *matter,* and it takes skill to *craft* conversations that count.

What Is a C.R.A.F.T. Conversation?

What is a C.R.A.F.T. conversation? As presented at the start of this chapter, our definition is simple:

> A skillful formal or informal oral exchange to explore perspectives and ideas, uncover misconceptions, and collaboratively problem-solve in a *c*lear, *r*ealistic, *a*ppropriate, *f*lexible, and *t*imely fashion; a conversation that does one or more of the following: builds capacity, invokes change, promotes collaboration, prioritizes celebration

When you think of the word *craft* or *crafting*, a conversation is most likely not the first thing that pops into your mind. You might picture a Pinterest board full of DIY projects or a store like Hobby Lobby or Michaels. You might even picture yourself cleaning up a mess from the kitchen table! To understand what a C.R.A.F.T. conversation is, we must start by defining the word *craft* and the word *conversation*.

Craft can be defined as an activity requiring skill or as skill in carrying out one's work. The key word here is *skill*. A *conversation* could be defined as an opportunity either between two people or among members of a small group that involves an oral exchange to explore perspectives and ideas, uncover misconceptions, and collaboratively problem-solve. The key phrase here is *oral exchange.* A C.R.A.F.T. conversation is on a totally different level than a casual conversation. In terms of *skill,* it's going to take some practice to get it right. In terms of *oral exchange,* it's time for some face-to-face discussion—and we don't mean FaceTime! As we begin describing the work of crafting conversations, the acronym C.R.A.F.T. illustrates the key points for leaders to focus on in cultivating their skills:

- *C* = Clear
- *R* = Realistic
- *A* = Appropriate
- *F* = Flexible
- *T* = Timely

Clear

It's important to present ideas, thoughts, or concerns clearly and concisely. In other words, do not be vague or evasive, and do not muddy the waters with extraneous information. C.R.A.F.T. conversations are always *clear* and to the point. Feedback within your conversations should be specific. Even though it's nice to hear "Great job," teachers want to know exactly what they did that was so great. Does a teacher need improvement? Let the teacher know what specifically needs to improve. Also, make sure your purpose is clearly set before beginning the conversation. It's hard to make a conversation count when you don't know why you are having it in the first place. When a conversation is clear, teachers and leaders can be fully present, and everyone leaves the conversation knowing exactly what needs to happen next.

Realistic

C.R.A.F.T. conversations are always *realistic* and should never paint a picture that is not accurate. In other words, be honest; be real.

A popular misconception is that honesty and respect can't always go together, especially when the feedback is not going to be easy to hear. Wrong! Honesty doesn't have to be brutal, as the popular perception suggests. This book will show you how honesty and respect can go hand in hand—and how they can play a critical role in teacher growth, your professional relationships, and outcomes for kids.

Be prepared to discuss concrete examples of what you have observed. You should also offer specific suggestions and discuss practical, realistic next steps, including some that your colleague can take right away. However, you must be sure to leave room for choice and for the teacher to have a voice. For instance, let's say you have a teacher with a classroom management issue. Give the teacher some options for next steps. Always ask yourself, "What is within this teacher's reach at this time?" If you have a teacher who is struggling to complete lesson plans from day to day, is it realistic to expect him to implement formative instructional practices right away? Think about each teacher as an individual and let that thought guide you. Goals and action steps should be individualized.

Appropriate

C.R.A.F.T. conversations are *appropriate* and tailored to the individual teacher. Consider the factors that may affect your conversation. Is this a first-year teacher you are preparing to converse with or is this a 20-year veteran? Is this teacher new to your school or has this teacher taught in the building for a long time? Expectations for each of these teachers would be different, and it is important to get to know the path each person has traveled to ensure your conversations are appropriate for each individual. Appropriateness also applies to the location of your conversation. Location is a key element that is often overlooked. Having the conversation in your office versus the teacher's classroom changes the mood and tone before anyone even speaks.

Flexible

When does a conversation occur? Make sure you consider the teacher's schedule and not just your own. When considering a time for conversations, make sure you never overlook the fact that a day in the life of a teacher is driven, in many cases, by a schedule you likely had a part in creating. If you gave the teacher one planning period to prepare three lessons, perhaps your conversations shouldn't take place during that planning period each time you meet.

When a teacher asks, "Do you have a minute?" take the time to listen if you can, or take the opportunity to schedule a meeting when your schedule allows you to give full attention to the teacher. It is important to be *flexible* during C.R.A.F.T. conversations. Sometimes your intended purpose is overshadowed by events beyond the control of the teacher, such as a sick child at home; or perhaps during the conversation you discover the teacher does not understand how to unpack a standard. It is perfectly fine to change the direction of a conversation, and in many instances, it is advantageous to do so on the spot.

Timely

C.R.A.F.T. conversations should always be current and *timely*. If you are having a conversation in April, you should not begin by discussing issues from December. It is important not to wait too long to have conversations with teachers. If you notice something on Monday, don't wait two months to discuss it.

Think about what you are trying to communicate to individual teachers. What is the most important and most urgent information to share? This consideration helps to ensure that your conversations are focused and not too lengthy. After all, one thing that teachers and leaders don't have is the luxury of being able to waste time.

Meeting the Challenge of the C.R.A.F.T. Criteria

Take a moment to reflect on one of the conversations you recently had with one of your teachers. Was it *c*lear, *r*ealistic, *a*ppropriate, *f*lexible, *and t*imely? It can be challenging to ensure that your conversations meet all the criteria, but through careful planning and reflection, these criteria will become an inherent part of your leadership and communication style. Now that you are familiar with the acronym, it's time to further explore the meaning of C.R.A.F.T. conversations and how they can transform your interactions and communication with your staff.

The Four Cornerstones of C.R.A.F.T. Conversations

Many school leaders spend thousands of dollars on professional development each year because they know that the success of any school is heavily dependent on its teachers. Although trainings, workshops, and PLCs help teachers gather new information and develop their skills, conversations also can lead toward improved teacher quality and efficacy that can support school growth.

Leaders engage teachers in conversation on a daily basis for myriad reasons—for example, to understand a student's behavior, to discuss the budget for an upcoming field trip, or to get up to speed on a parental concern. Many of these conversations are short and focused, with little need for follow-up. C.R.A.F.T. conversations, by contrast, are specifically designed to help leaders with their work in four foundational areas: Building Capacity, Invoking Change, Promoting Collaboration, and Prioritizing Celebration. When you think of a cornerstone, you may visualize the strong foundation of a building or other structure. That's exactly why we refer to these foundational pieces of a C.R.A.F.T. conversation as *cornerstones*. They are designed to create a strong, lasting foundation that can lead to positive and sustainable change in your building.

Building Capacity

Consider the range of teacher experience in schools. Some teachers might be novices, just beginning their careers in the field, whereas others are proud to call themselves veterans. With the wide range of teacher experience present in most schools and constantly changing standards, leaders must ask themselves, "How can we really support teachers at every level?" Building capacity focuses on meeting teachers where they are. C.R.A.F.T. conversations allow leaders to tailor discussions to individual needs, so all teachers can feel supported, valued for what they bring to the table, and ready to take their practice to the next level.

Invoking Change

Every school faces its own challenges, such as declines in student achievement, low teacher retention rates, or lack of parental involvement. No matter what the issues might be, leaders continually set goals and lean on their staff to bring about change. C.R.A.F.T. conversations promote change by encouraging a deeper look at the context surrounding challenging situations. Who are our students? What is happening in our school community? Failure to understand context leads to an inability to change. C.R.A.F.T. conversations also allow for a more intentional understanding of teachers' mindsets. By understanding what teachers believe and what drives them as individuals, leaders can determine how they can best support the changes that are necessary for school success.

Promoting Collaboration

Take a moment to think about your own style of working with others. Do you ask for input on tasks, or do you just decide on something and that's the way it is? Before making big decisions, do you take time to engage in conversations with stakeholders or to brainstorm and strategize with your teachers? Collaboration should be at the heart of everything that goes on in your building. That's why C.R.A.F.T. conversations are designed to model collaboration by ensuring that leaders and teachers engage in conversations as "thought partners" and codesigners of next steps. C.R.A.F.T. conversations do not rely on top-down directives. Instead, they focus on working alongside teachers to achieve goals. Even as leaders plan for follow-up at the close of a conversation, collaborative opportunities should be at the forefront. Whether teachers move on to peer observations or coplanning sessions with instructional coaches, the idea is to remove teachers from their silos. As a leader, it's important that you "walk the walk" yourself, so be sure to look for collaborative opportunities and give your staff space and time to work as a team.

Prioritizing Celebration

Principals, assistant principals, and teacher leaders often embark on the arduous task of making their school a place where teachers want to be on a daily basis and where they want to stay for the long run. Crafting honest conversations that celebrate small and big successes is one way to achieve this goal. As leaders with many responsibilities and busy schedules, it is so easy for us to forget to celebrate. Once a goal is achieved, we often move on to the next one without taking time to pause, reflect, and pat ourselves on the back. Worst of all, we forget to take a moment to recognize our teachers for their hard work. C.R.A.F.T. conversations remind leaders of the importance of celebrating teachers for their achievements in ways that are authentic and meaningful.

Why the Cornerstones Are Important

C.R.A.F.T. conversations can do many things, but we believe that they are most effective in helping leaders build capacity, invoke change, promote collaboration, and prioritize celebration. At first glance, this might seem like an abbreviated list. However, the success of your school most likely hinges on one or more of the four cornerstones. Remember that these cornerstones are designed to create a solid foundation that can lead to positive and sustainable change in your building. These four foundational pieces of C.R.A.F.T. conversations, when addressed comprehensively, can help school leaders garner the results and outcomes they desire.

Key Components of a C.R.A.F.T. Conversation

Now that you know what a C.R.A.F.T. conversation is and have discovered why such conversations matter in your school, it's time to look at the anatomy of a C.R.A.F.T. conversation. A C.R.A.F.T. conversation has six main components:

- Planning
- Opening
- Engaging
- Closing
- Reflecting
- Following up

As you work through these components, remember to reflect continuously on the C.R.A.F.T. acronym. It is valuable to think about these components in a cyclical manner, realizing that the opportunity to revisit and reexamine the intent, impact, and outcome of the conversation is always present. Figure 1.1 shows the key components of a C.R.A.F.T. conversation and reminds us that the nature of such conversations is cyclical.

FIGURE 1.1

Key Components of a C.R.A.F.T. Conversation

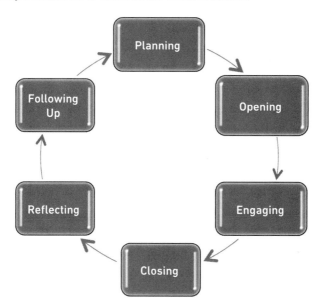

Planning

The first component of a C.R.A.F.T. conversation is planning. Think about when you actually craft an item such as a gingerbread house or a scrapbook. It all starts with a plan. First, you might visualize the final product or possibly search online for inspiration. Next, you might make a list of the materials needed and possibly set a budget before heading to the store. Regardless of what steps you take, you plan. C.R.A.F.T. conversations are no different. You must have a plan.

For many leaders, planning will start with careful consideration of school goals. What matters most in your building? Is it increasing student achievement, closing the achievement gap between specific groups of students, or maybe even creating and sustaining a positive culture? For others, the focus will be on the individual teacher. What's going on in the classroom? No matter where you choose to begin, planning for C.R.A.F.T. conversations does not require linear organization; rather, it thrives on an organic collection of thoughts, considerations, lists, and reminders.

It is important to note that even with a plan, sometimes things go awry. For example, let's say you "craft" your very first iMovie to capture footage from a family vacation. It might not turn out great the first time around, so you reflect, figure out your learning curve, make adjustments, and then try again. Your next iMovie turns out better than your first. Leaders should approach C.R.A.F.T. conversations the same way.

Opening

Once you have planned, it's time to act. Have you ever heard the saying "You only get one chance to make a first impression"? Leaders should think of the opening of a C.R.A.F.T. conversation in the same way. There are no do-overs, so it is important to start things off on a positive note. Although positivity is invaluable, there are many more things to consider. For example, have you already established rapport with this teacher? If not, take some time to get to know a little bit about the teacher's journey and share pieces of your own story.

Even when the time you have allotted for the conversation is short, opening with an opportunity to connect goes a long way. If you do have a specific time frame, establish that up front, and acknowledge that you may need to finish the conversation later if time gets away from you.

The opening of the conversation should also include a mutual understanding of your purpose and intent. The teacher should know exactly why the conversation is taking place before engaging. Sometimes it is best to take a straightforward approach and state the purpose directly. In other cases, this goal can be achieved by using inquiry. For example, you might ask, "What are you hoping to gain out of our time together today?" Regardless of the method chosen, all parties should know and understand from the very beginning the *why* behind the conversation.

Engaging

Engaging can be thought of as the meat and potatoes of the conversation; it's where the conversation actually *happens*. There are four things to focus on to achieve engagement: listening, inquiry, indicators, and expertise.

Listening is paramount. We are sure you have been a part of a conversation in which you felt as though the other person was listening only to respond. C.R.A.F.T. conversations call for *active* listening. Active listening requires you to listen with an open mind and to seek to understand the other person's point of view throughout the conversation.

Inquiry and *indicators* are additional pertinent pieces needed to ensure engagement is taking place. As a leader, you should ask open-ended and probing questions to provide teachers with an opportunity to expound on any of their thoughts or ideas. By asking questions, you are leveling the playing field and allowing teachers to have a prominent voice in every conversation. Indicators, which can be thought of as supporting artifacts, should help highlight the focus and purpose of the conversation. They should be current, clear, and selected with intention. When chosen carefully, indicators help teachers to better understand their practice and to see things as they are and not as teachers wish for them to be.

Expertise is also valuable. Leaders and teachers bring so much to the table, and both parties should feel comfortable sharing. Teachers should take the lead here because they know their own classroom better than anyone else. As a leader, you should refrain from trying to exert your expertise over and over again. When you do share your expertise, it should be focused and connected to the goal of the conversation. Be selective!

Closing

The end of a C.R.A.F.T. conversation is just as important as the beginning. The closing provides space to ensure that all parties leave the conversation with a mutual understanding of what was discussed and what needs to happen next. To close, you might ask the teacher to summarize the critical points from the conversation, or it might be necessary for you to lay out expectations in a bullet-point format. As you close, teachers should agree that the intended purpose has been met and should understand that it is a priority for you to continue working as a partner with them as they make strides toward their goals. Last, always thank teachers for their time.

Reflecting

As school leaders, we can be tempted to move from one conversation to the next without pausing to reflect. However, reflection is key to improving your C.R.A.F.T. conversation skills. The great thing about reflection is that there really is no right or wrong way to get the job done. Some might choose to journal, and others might ask themselves a few questions, such as "What went well during today's conversation?" or "What type of professional learning opportunity would be best for this teacher?" The important thing is to take time to think about the conversation and the work ahead.

Reflection provides a tremendous amount of self-awareness, but it accomplishes nothing if leaders do not act on it. Let's say you have been reflecting on two conversations, and you notice that in both cases you did 90 percent of the talking. It might be time to think about the types of questions you are asking, or perhaps you need to work on making sure you are setting the right tone during the opening. Reflection also provides you with an opportunity to think about the work the teacher has done thus far. What is working and what is not? Why? It might be time to try something new or to get extra support from teacher leaders in your building. Reflection and action go hand in hand when it comes to making every C.R.A.F.T. conversation better than your last.

Following Up

Once the conversation has come to a close and you have taken time to reflect, there is still important work to do. Following up can look very different depending on the purpose of the conversation, and follow-up should always be tailored to the individual teacher and the desired outcomes. In one situation, follow-up could be as simple as a meeting in two weeks to review quiz data. At other times, you might ask a teacher to videotape a lesson so the two of you can watch it together and discuss independent and mutual observations. The key is to ensure that the follow-up activities are directly aligned to the goals you both set.

Following up shows teachers that you are invested in their growth, and it provides the additional support and accountability that many teachers want and need. It also models collaboration and allows teachers to see you as not only a leader but also as a coach or mentor. Just as a gold medalist "sticks the landing" to score a perfect 10, you can go home with the gold by following up. If you have a conversation and you choose not to follow up, you have wasted time, and more than likely you will not see the change that needs to occur. Take the time. Stick to it. You will not regret it.

Remember the vignette presented at the beginning of the chapter? Let's follow the new assistant principal, Monica, and the first-year, alternatively certified teacher, Jennifer, as they embark upon a C.R.A.F.T. conversation. As the person assigned to developing teacher quality, Monica has considered the components of C.R.A.F.T. conversations and is ready to execute her plan. She welcomes Jennifer into her office after lunch.

Monica: First of all, welcome to our school. We are so excited that you decided to join our team! Tell me a little bit about your journey to becoming a teacher.

Jennifer: This is my first job teaching, and I'm very excited! I have an undergrad degree in biology and just decided that I wanted to teach. I haven't had any intro education courses. I'm in one now, and I'm having a hard time getting started since I've never done this before. My mom and grandmother were both teachers, so I guess you could say it's in my blood. But I'm totally at a loss as to where to begin for an opening script, and I'm not really sure of the purpose. I guess I just thought it would come naturally when my students walked in the door the first day of school.

Monica: Well, I'm so glad we connected today. I have some great resources for you to consider as you work on developing your script for the first day of school. Developing a script allows you to anticipate a variety of situations that may come up. The script also allows you to address some critical areas that must be presented up front to your students to set the tone for the entire school year.

Jennifer: I didn't really think about how the first day could affect my whole year.

Monica: Let me ask you a few questions so I have a better understanding of your assignment. First, do you know what your professor was trying to achieve through this assignment, and second, what is the purpose of having a script?

Jennifer: I really wasn't sure until just now! You mentioned setting the tone for the entire year. I didn't really think about what a critical day it is.

Monica: I think you are thinking about a script too literally, and that's not surprising given the wording of the assignment. You certainly will not pull out this script and start reading it to your students! That would be very unnatural.

Jennifer: OK. I'm glad you clarified that. It really hadn't been presented that way in class.

Monica: I have some resources for you to look through that will give you a laundry list of things to prepare for on the first day of school. What are some things you can think of right off that would be important to address?

Jennifer: I guess where the students will sit would be important.

Monica: Yes! And routines! That's exactly what you need to think about. From the moment you greet them at the door, how will they know what to do? Beginning-of-class routines— what they do before the bell rings, then when the bell rings, how and where students turn in assignments. These are all so important to establish right up front.

Jennifer: That seems like a lot for the first day.

Monica: You're right, and so you need to think of how you will establish routines as they come up throughout the first few weeks of school. For instance, you aren't going to establish a routine for student collaboration until the need for it occurs. And safety rules and procedures won't be addressed until your first lab.

Jennifer: That really makes a lot of sense now.

As Monica flips through the books she had pulled out to lend to Jennifer, she points out and bookmarks several sections with specifics about planning for the first days of school. She also gives Jennifer her personal cell phone number and encourages her to call if she gets stuck or needs some additional guidance as she finalizes her assignment.

Monica: I hope that these resources are helpful to you as you plan for your assignment and as you take time to develop your script for that first day. I would love to visit your classroom on the first day of school if that's OK with you, and I'd be happy to read through your assignment before you submit it as well.

Jennifer: Oh, that would be great!

Monica: When you finish your assignment over the weekend, send it to me. I'll review it Sunday evening and offer suggestions. Let's also plan to meet next Wednesday morning after the faculty meeting. I can help you think through the plan you developed so you can effectively put it into action over the first few days and weeks of school.

Jennifer: Do you really have time to do all of that? I know you have a lot of teachers assigned to work with this year.

Monica: Of course! I'm here to support you, and I want you to feel free to reach out to me whenever you need to. It won't all be on you, though, so just know that I'll be visiting your classroom frequently and following up each time I visit. Stop by, text me, or shoot me an e-mail anytime.

Jennifer: You can count on that for sure! I think these resources and our conversation have really given me direction, and I know I can get this done pretty easily now. I had *no* direction from my professor!

Monica: Sometimes your best resources are in your school. Don't forget that there is a network of support for you here that extends beyond the classroom, and I'm a big part of that. So, what do you see as your next steps moving forward?

Jennifer: First, I'm going to read through these resources and make a list of important topics and items to address on the first days of school, emphasizing routines. Once my script is developed, I'll e-mail it to you by Sunday afternoon. Then

I'll plan on meeting with you next Wednesday after the faculty meeting so we can talk about any follow-up questions I have.

Monica: Perfect! I look forward to reading your work and meeting with you next Wednesday. Please reach out between now and then if you have any questions along the way—you have my cell phone number now.

Jennifer: I promise I will! Thanks so much for your time and for the great resources. I'll see you at the afternoon closing session later today.

Monica takes some time to reflect after the conversation. "How receptive was Jennifer to my suggestions?" she wonders. "Did I actively listen?" Monica remembers she had offered to read Jennifer's paper before it is submitted, so she drafts a quick e-mail to reiterate her willingness to help. Monica also thinks about her offer to follow up by visiting Jennifer's classroom on the first day of school. She quickly blocks off 30 minutes on her calendar for a visit. There is only one first day of school, she thinks, and she can't miss her visit to Jennifer's room.

The opening vignette and closing dialogues in Chapters 1 through 6 offer examples of authentic C.R.A.F.T. conversations. The example just presented highlights the start of a new school year and shows how C.R.A.F.T. conversations can be useful before a single student enters the building. Maybe you are beginning this book in the late fall or even early spring, and the first day of school is behind you. Don't worry! It's never too late to connect with your teachers and offer support. C.R.A.F.T. conversations are one effective way to do so. As you read the vignettes and closing dialogues in the coming chapters, some may seem unrealistic when you consider your particular school and teachers. We ask that you consider each vignette and conversation presented as it relates to the content of each chapter and reflect on how you might move forward to positively influence *your* students, *your* teachers, and *your* school community through C.R.A.F.T. conversations.

Closing Thoughts

Are you ready to delve deeper into the skill of crafting conversations that count in your school? Think of this book as professional learning on demand! Whenever you are ready, this book will help you reflect on your own practices as a school leader and help you to become a skilled C.R.A.F.T. conversationalist. With the basics we have presented in Chapter 1, you should now have a foundational understanding of C.R.A.F.T. conversations and why there is a need for crafting conversations that count in schools.

Chapter 2 will dedicate a section to each of the four cornerstones briefly examined in this chapter. We will walk you through each cornerstone to provide you with the *why* behind the need for such a skill. C.R.A.F.T. conversations should always be *about* something, and the two questions you should be able to answer after a C.R.A.F.T. conversation are "Which of the cornerstones did I address?" and "Why was this (or why were these) the most significant cornerstone(s) to address?"

2

What Can C.R.A.F.T. Conversations Really Do?

Conversation isn't about proving a point; true conversation is about going on a journey with the people you are speaking with.

—Ricky Maye, American author

INSIDE THIS CHAPTER:

The Four Cornerstones—
- Building Capacity
- Invoking Change
- Promoting Collaboration
- Prioritizing Celebration

Assistant principal Luis has been assigned to evaluate the department chairs at his new school. At the beginning of the year, it is really important for him to get to know each of them individually. He sets up one-on-one conferences and makes sure to visit each of their classrooms a few times during the first few weeks of school. The quality feedback he provides starts a mutual back-and-forth exchange with most of the department chairs during the first few months of the school year.

Luis's focus is on building strong, trusting relationships. He needs to know where each teacher's individual strengths are so he can focus his work for the second part of the school year. Through conversations, observations, and participation in meetings, he concludes that the members of this group are certainly dynamic individually, but there is much work to be done to help them build capacity within their own departments.

The time for midyear conferences is quickly approaching as the semester comes to a close. As Luis plans for the meetings, he reflects on each of the four cornerstones and each component of a C.R.A.F.T. conversation.

For years, leaders have focused on improving their schools via traditional methods such as conferences, professional development sessions, professional learning communities, and peer observations. Although these strategies can be effective, they tend to happen only once a month or, in many cases, once a year, offering cookie-cutter approaches with little to no individualization. So how can leaders build better schools on a more consistent basis and in a personalized manner? Focusing on the four cornerstones of C.R.A.F.T. conversations—Building Capacity, Invoking Change, Promoting Collaboration, and Prioritizing Celebration—is an excellent way to begin.

The Embedded Nature of the Four Cornerstones

Although each of the four cornerstones can stand on its own, something magical happens when they are working in concert. Figure 2.1 illustrates the four cornerstones and reminds us they are nested to build upon one another.

Keeping in mind the visual presented in Figure 2.1, reflect on how each of these cornerstones is represented within your school. Which cornerstone is a strength, and which is an area of opportunity?

FIGURE 2.1

The Four Cornerstones of C.R.A.F.T. Conversations

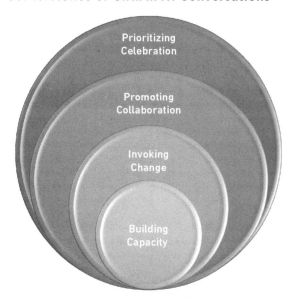

How can you influence your teachers and change your school for the better by focusing on these four cornerstones? You may be thinking that there isn't anything that really needs to change in your school. Perhaps each cornerstone is fully practiced in your building. Even so, there are things to be keenly aware of as you begin to understand how each cornerstone influences the others.

Notice in Figure 2.1 that Building Capacity is at the core. Everything starts with the individual. The capacity of every single person in your school counts. First, you need to identify who the leaders are and begin to work with them to build or enhance their capacity as leaders. If this effort is already a part of your school's core business, then stop to think about how you promote and build the capacity of the other faculty and staff. Are you missing an element that could strengthen your grade-level teams? Have you overlooked the paraprofessionals? These are just two examples of groups that may need some attention. The idea is to ensure that every individual in your school is growing and developing.

Once you have begun to build capacity throughout your school, it becomes easier to begin addressing the second cornerstone, Invoking

Change. A commitment to improvement always involves some element of change. Change is sometimes deemed a corrective measure to make things better, but that is not necessarily the case. More often, change is something that is inevitable if we truly intend to prepare our students for the world beyond their formal education. For example, change can simply mean moving your school into a more digitally oriented frame of mind. Have you heard of schools going paperless? How about a school where students who are on track academically stay home every six weeks for a digital learning day? Neither of these changes is punitive or taking place because a teacher has done something wrong. Instead, these changes provide a more responsible and digitally aware environment that will better prepare students for the world beyond the brick-and-mortar school walls. Although these examples are of large-scale changes, the same thought process can be applied when thinking about individual teachers. Even your best teachers can become better.

Change doesn't occur easily without collective effort. Journal article highlights on LinkedIn or other news sources often relay corporations' need for their employees and leaders to work well together. Collaboration is key! As a leader, the cornerstone of Promoting Collaboration must be at the top of your mind as you help your staff continually work together to move your building to the next level.

This effort is less about carving out time for collaboration and more about improving and expanding the ways in which collaboration happens. For example, let's consider the iGen—those individuals born in the mid-1990s to early 2000s. Like the millennials, this group of learners has never known a world without internet access. The terrorist attacks on September 11 are not part of their *memory*; they are a part of *history*. Members of the iGen are not necessarily all tech savvy, but they are tech dependent. As this generation enters the teaching profession, how might methods of collaboration evolve? Again, you may be thinking that collaboration is something your school does well. If so, then you are in a pivotal position to examine how you can expand collaboration at a deeper level.

When people are working together toward a goal, there will definitely be something to celebrate! Some schools do a great job with the fourth cornerstone, Prioritizing Celebration, throughout the school year, because it is woven into the fabric of the school. This practice goes back to how leaders choose to build staff unity and what some call their "school family." Typically, schools conduct various celebrations, but often we need to change not only *how* we celebrate but also *what* we celebrate when it comes to our teachers. For instance, have you ever celebrated teachers' authentic use of a new instructional strategy? Does the concept of celebrating your 7th grade team for initiating student-led conferences sound foreign to you? As you begin to take the lead in celebrating success, the practice will infectiously spread to create an environment in which your teachers recognize achievement and celebrate the great things going on before you get the chance to do so.

Digging Deeper into the Four Cornerstones

Now that you have a general understanding of each of the four cornerstones, it is important to further explore each one individually. Although the cornerstones work in concert, leaders often find the need to isolate one cornerstone at a time, particularly when working with individual teachers. As each cornerstone is discussed, ask yourself two questions: "What does this currently look like at my school?" and "How can I promote growth in this area individually and collectively?"

Building Capacity

If you walked into any school, you likely would find teachers at various places in their careers. Some may be in the midst of their first year in the field. A few may have just finished their fourth year in the classroom and are questioning whether teaching will be their lifelong career path. Perhaps a handful are only a few years from retirement. Regardless of where teachers fall on the career continuum, leaders face the challenge of continuously developing all of them as professionals. In other words, leaders are charged with building capacity—the act of intentionally enhancing one's actual or potential ability to perform.

As a school leader, nothing is more important than ensuring that your teachers continue to learn and grow. One would think that teachers would be automatic lifelong learners, making their own development a top priority. However, when you factor in lesson planning, club advising, parent-teacher conferences, tutoring, grading papers, analyzing data, coaching, and a lengthy list of additional teacher duties and responsibilities, it is easy to see how some teachers' individual learning gets pushed further and further down on the priority list.

Building capacity is the linchpin for the other three cornerstones. First, it is the foundation for the other three cornerstones. Second, it really could be considered the single most important part of a school leader's job. Building capacity is a task in which every leader should want to be 100 percent hands-on. However, in many cases it is the exact opposite—leaders hire "experts" or call on educators inside their building to coach teachers. Although this distributed leadership approach can be beneficial, it is ultimately the leader's responsibility to make professional growth and development a top priority for all staff members, regardless of their years in the field or prior performance.

Building capacity is the core of our cornerstones for three specific reasons: (1) it highlights teacher growth and development as an expectation; (2) it acknowledges teachers as unique individuals; and (3) it serves as the foundation for school success and sustainability. Let's look at each of these more closely.

A focus on building capacity makes it clear to all teachers that growth and development are not only valued but expected. We have all heard about or worked in schools where it is perfectly fine to remain stagnant as long as your test scores are high and parents aren't complaining. Teachers can stay in their bubbles while using the same plans, strategies, and even assessments year after year. Think about how easy it is for leaders to have a mindset of "If it ain't broke, don't fix it." It saves time and energy! However, if leaders want successful schools that are prepared to take on the ever-changing educational landscape, their teachers must be ready and willing to learn new things. Whether it is downloading and learning about a popular new app that can be used for a project or taking courses to earn advanced placement certification, all teachers should be advancing their own knowledge in order to do the same for students.

The Building Capacity cornerstone also helps leaders to acknowledge each teacher as an individual. We hear the phrase "One size does not fit all" over and over in education. Typically, we think about this when discussing classroom strategies for students, but what about our teachers? Most people tend to think of capacity as it relates to one's skill level or knowledge. This is an important part of capacity because it speaks to a person's individual strengths and areas of opportunity as well. What does this person know and what is he or she able to do *today?* To build capacity, you must first meet people where they are. With teachers, however, you also need to think about capacity in terms of roles and responsibilities. For instance, during football season, your U.S. history teacher who also coaches football might have a lower level of capacity. Your math department chair who just returned to work after being out on maternity leave with her first child might have a different level of capacity than she did last year.

Building capacity is also the foundation for school success and sustainability. If you did a case study of highly successful schools, you would probably discover that teachers in those schools are continuously learning. They are reading books, participating in lesson studies, conducting peer observations, reflecting on videos of their class, and more. They have an intentional focus on perfecting their instructional skills and acumen. Building capacity in this way helps schools to become successful and stay that way.

Invoking Change

We have all heard the saying "The only thing constant is change," and that has never been truer than in the field of education. Something is always changing, whether it is state mandates, grading methods, or school policies. Given that change is constant, we might assume that teachers have grown comfortable with it. However, in many schools, change might as well be a four-letter word.

The negativity surrounding change in education is complex in its causes, but much of it has to do with changes made that are not in the best interest of students. But what about the changes that *are* in the best interest of students but prove to be uncomfortable or arduous for the adults involved? Leaders have a responsibility to support teachers through such changes.

Lasting change does not typically just happen. It takes a deep understanding of why the change is needed and buy-in from various stakeholders—especially school leaders and teachers. The most important point for leaders to realize is that they cannot do things on their own. Sure, some leaders use scare tactics to force change. But that method is completely ineffective and puts long-term success out of reach. If the change is warranted and is best for students, leaders must focus on helping teachers navigate through the change until it becomes an embedded part of their practice. Invoking change is the act of intentionally bringing about a different position, course of action, or direction.

Invoking change is important for three reasons: (1) it places an emphasis on contextual understanding; (2) it encourages leaders to focus on teachers' mindsets; and (3) it acknowledges challenges in a solution-oriented manner. Let's examine each of these in turn.

The first step in bringing about change in schools is contextual understanding. For lasting change to happen, leaders must take time to reflect. The discipline problems you are seeing in a veteran teacher's classroom didn't happen overnight. The school culture wasn't amazing on Monday and terrifying by Tuesday. What brought you to this point? Who were the key stakeholders involved? By understanding the context that surrounds a school's challenges and focus areas, leaders can begin to fully ascertain why change is necessary. Once leaders understand the *why*, it is much easier to begin to brainstorm possible solutions. Contextual understanding helps to focus leaders' energy and makes it easier for them to help teachers understand the need for change and how the change is going to make for a better school and community.

Once teachers understand the *why* and the *how*, only one thing can hold them back from making the change: their mindsets. *Mindset* refers to one's mental attitude or inclination and can be one of the most powerful factors when it comes to change. For instance, Ingrid understands that she needs to find other ways to assess her students besides multiple-choice, paper-and-pencil exams. She knows how to assess in other ways, such as through the use of portfolios and one-on-one conversations with her students, but what does Ingrid believe internally about assessments? Is her mindset more traditional, leading her to think, "I took paper-and-pencil tests, and I turned out just fine," or is she thinking, "Portfolios take too much time to grade"? School leaders must understand their teachers' mindsets, particularly for those teachers who are finding it difficult to change. With this understanding, leaders are able to provide the additional support necessary to shift certain mindsets to make change possible.

Every school has its own unique challenges. Whether dealing with financial constraints, low graduation rates, or high student mobility, school leaders must take the lead by facing challenges head on. In most cases, overcoming challenges involves change. Leaders who seek to invoke change approach challenges in a thoughtful, solutions-oriented manner. They start by gathering information to understand the challenge and always involve others as they brainstorm possible solutions. When it is time to bring about change in their building, buy-in becomes easier because they are able to confidently help teachers understand the *why* while presenting solutions and a possible course of action. Teachers respect leaders who do not shirk from challenges and who are attentive in how they bring their faculty along on the journey.

Promoting Collaboration

When you think of the phrase "promoting collaboration," what comes to mind? Our definition of this cornerstone is simple: promoting collaboration is the act of intentionally helping others work together toward a common goal.

Some leaders do not focus on collaboration. They let their staff members self-select how they want to work. This approach is a mistake. Other leaders provide teachers with time to collaborate but do not give much attention to how collaboration takes place during the time allotted. This approach is also not advantageous. Collaboration should be the heartbeat of any school, and teachers should be provided with the time and resources to collaborate effectively.

Collaboration is also directly linked to communication. Can you think of an example of an excellent collaborator who is a poor communicator? Collaboration and communication are each other's yin and yang. As a school leader, it is important for you to recognize your role in the implementation of this dual-natured cornerstone. When you accept the charge to promote collaboration, you are also taking responsibility for improving communication in your school.

Have you heard of an individual or a group within an organization working in a "silo"? Think of the old silos that may now stand abandoned and rusted along the sides of country backroads. They are relics of the past. At one time it may have been common and acceptable for school leaders and teachers to work in silos, and they may have been able to produce adequate results with their students. Now, the demand to provide world-class educational settings cannot be accomplished by just one person. Collaboration is key in today's society, and the power of *we* is certainly stronger than the power of *me*. Everyone must be able to work in teams and groups to reach common organizational goals. There is power in multiple voices and perspectives, and embracing collaboration means everyone's thoughts and ideas are valued.

Promoting collaboration is important for three specific reasons: (1) it provides for a more inclusive and innovative work environment; (2) it ensures more consistent implementation of best practices throughout the school; and (3) it saves teachers time and energy. Let's look at each of these more closely.

Are your school day and master schedule designed to allow teachers to work together more inclusively? To collaborate and to share innovative practices, teachers must have time built into the school day, and such time must be monitored. Once teachers have the time to collaborate, new ideas and new ways to reach students abound. The ways in which teachers collaborate tend to develop as well. You will find that teachers are not just sitting around chatting and drinking coffee. Instead, they are using creative protocols and engaging in preparatory work to make their time together meaningful. When collaborative practices are the school norm, teachers feel a part of something bigger than just what happens in their classrooms.

As teachers begin to use collaboration more and more, the implementation of best practices becomes more consistent throughout the school. A great way to see this effect in action is to schedule your classroom visits and walkthroughs for a specific subject or grade level on the same day. For example, if you are curious about how the 3rd grade literature teachers are implementing a new reading strategy, plan to visit each one on the same day to get a clear picture of what's going on from classroom to classroom. Teachers who collaborate seem to have a higher sense of accountability. They feel compelled to use schoolwide instructional strategies when they know they will be discussing the implementation of them with their colleagues. Collaboration provides a safe place for teachers to discuss what worked, what didn't work, and what the team plans to change moving forward.

When you think about promoting collaboration, remember that all teachers come to the table with a specific skill set, offering a diverse pot of skills to draw from. Which teammate is an expert in making instructional videos for a flipped classroom? Who is really great at developing rubrics for projects? Teachers begin to share the load, which allows them to spend more time doing the things that they are passionate about. Distributed leadership begins to happen at the micro level as teachers realize that there is strength in numbers. They will soon appreciate the amount of time and energy that is saved when everyone is working together toward a common goal.

Prioritizing Celebration

If you are reading this book, there's a chance that you were a Teacher of the Year—or at least know somebody who was. The coveted Teacher of the Year award, or TOTY, is typically given near the end of the school year to a teacher who had a particularly successful year. The recipient is usually honored with some type of celebration and receives a nice plaque or trophy. Right now you may be asking yourself, "Is there something wrong with the TOTY award?" No! However, when you work in a school with 85 teachers, you have to ask yourself, "When did I celebrate the other 84 teachers in my building?"

Schools are incredibly busy places. There's always a program, a special presentation, or a conference. Add in board meetings, evaluations, and district planning sessions, and it's a wonder that leaders find time to celebrate teachers, even at the end of the year. Celebrating your teachers may seem like something that doesn't need to be prioritized, but it is one of the best things you can do for staff morale and school culture. To ensure that a celebration is authentic and meaningful, it has to be something that a leader focuses attention on. For us, prioritizing celebration is the act of intentionally honoring teachers' work on an ongoing basis.

Often when we hear the word *celebrate*, we think of a showy gesture. Maybe some balloons? A cake? A banner? But who said celebrations always have to be big and for all to see? Honoring the work of teachers in meaningful ways could involve small gestures such as writing a thank-you note and attaching it to the teacher's favorite candy bar, or communicating the three ways you have seen the teacher engage parents during a one-on-one meeting. Both ways of celebrating say, "I see you!" and "Job well done!"

So what exactly should you celebrate? There's really nothing off limits. The important thing is to make sure the gesture is authentic. There is no need to hunt for something to celebrate in your building, and you do not need to celebrate every teacher every day. If you are in classrooms daily and tuned in to what is going on in your school, causes for celebration will find you. It is also valuable to celebrate things that align with your school goals or annual theme. Are you focused on data? Find ways to celebrate teachers who are using their data in innovative ways. Is your theme this year all about culture? Look for teachers who are changing the culture in small ways.

Prioritizing celebration is imperative for three reasons: (1) it helps leaders focus on what teachers are doing right; (2) it honors success both big and small; and (3) it values teachers' work throughout the school year. Let's take a closer look at each of these.

It is incredibly easy to call out what people are doing wrong—particularly when leaders find themselves stuck in "evaluator mode."

Leaders who prioritize celebration are looking for what their teachers are doing right! Teaching is a challenging profession, with highs and lows and everything in between. Intentionally focusing on the things that are going well and being done at the highest level makes for a positive culture and should bring any leader a great deal of joy. Often such joy can be infectious, leading to an environment in which teachers are also eager to celebrate one another. When celebration shifts away from being top-down and becomes embedded in your staff's behavior, you have made your school a place where teachers want to be.

You probably have been invited to some of those big, once-in-a-lifetime celebrations—like when your best friend turned 40 or your parents celebrated their 25th wedding anniversary. The "biggies" are always fun to celebrate, even at school. Who doesn't like to celebrate those teachers with perfect attendance or those who had 95 percent or more of their class exceed the standards on the state assessment? These moments are important, and teachers should be honored for their work. However, leaders must be careful not to forget to celebrate the small things as well. What about the teacher who had 70 percent of her classroom parents show up at STEAM night when the school average was only 10 percent? How about the group of 4th grade teachers who started their own PLC around effective homework practices? Leaders should focus on celebrating all wins, both large and small.

As mentioned earlier, there is nothing wrong with a TOTY award. That's a perfectly good way to celebrate a teacher. However, leaders must focus on celebrating teachers in their building throughout the year. Doing so helps to acknowledge all of the things teachers do month to month and day to day to make student success possible. It also encourages leaders to celebrate a large variety of teachers in their building.

Let's revisit the vignette presented at the beginning of the chapter. Because Building Capacity is the core cornerstone of C.R.A.F.T. conversations, let's see how Luis hones in on this area as he leads his midyear group conference with the department lead teachers.

Luis has only one hour to communicate a large amount of information, so he sends a few questions in advance for group members to think about as the meeting time approaches. For the meeting, he has pieces of cardstock divided into four quadrants, with one of the following discussion questions printed in each box:

1. How do you build capacity with the teachers in your department?

2. How do you support changes that occur throughout the year in your department?

3. What are the collaborative practices you use in your department?

4. How do you celebrate milestones in your department?

Each teacher leader has two or three minutes to write responses in each of the quadrants. After the participants have filled in all four quadrants on their own cards, they do silent rotations to read the responses. Luis doesn't want to leave any of the four cornerstones out of the discussion, but he knows he needs to focus first on Building Capacity. The results are amazing! Here is a snippet of the conversation among the group members, in which they learn from one another to build their own skill sets.

Luis: Let's first focus our conversation on how each of you has been working to build capacity within your department and see what we can learn from one another that will create some momentum as we look toward next semester.

Brett: I'll go first. In the foreign language department, I have leads within each language, and then I go even deeper and have leads within each level. Looking through other responses, it seems like everyone may not be going as deep as I am, and maybe I'm wrong.

Luis: Who else wants to share or build upon what Brett has started our conversation with?

Shawnna: I think I'm guilty of trying to do everything for everyone, and I'm sometimes nervous about releasing leadership to others. I have very capable people in my department, but I think I try to do too much for them.

Luis: I think a lot of leaders are guilty of that sometimes, Shawnna. Does anyone else want to share how they work to build capacity within their department—to help Shawnna with a few ideas that she can start to implement in her department?

Evelyn: It has been a gradual thing for me. I know I'm still not there quite the way Brett is, but my teachers are divided into grade-level groups with leaders. I try to meet with that core group of leaders at least every other week to get a sense of how their teachers are working together collaboratively. If there is a teacher they are concerned about who may not be contributing or is bucking the direction the team is trying to go, I make a special effort to engage with that teacher over the next week to find a positive element in her practice and encourage her to share it with the group the next time they meet.

Shawnna: I like what you are doing with your core leaders, Evelyn, to help support their own capacity to lead. I get the complaint that some people are not pulling their weight, but I haven't really known what to do with that other than listen.

Carlton: I like that too, Evelyn. Next semester I'm going to start scheduling time to meet with my subgroup leaders more often and provide them with the opportunity to also learn from one another. With so many groups in the social studies department, I've been struggling to keep tabs on how each group is progressing.

Tracie: This may not be right, but I stepped down as a group leader this year so I could bounce from group to group. It's a blessing to have all of my math teachers with the same planning period this year. I did ask them to all agree upon one day out of the week to meet so I'm not so overwhelmed throughout the week with trying to get to all of the different meetings. I did that last year, and it ran me ragged.

Carlton: That's a great point, Tracie. I allowed each team to pick the best day for each group, and it ended up being four different days of the week. I can never get any of my own work done during the day. I think I'll ask them to all change to the same day of the week for second semester and see if that helps with my sanity.

Luis: That brings up a good point. Do we need to think about more consistent practices across curriculum areas that would allow you more time to help your groups build capacity?

Brett: I think that would help others move toward a model that even the other administrators could help us with. They try their best to visit our weekly meetings, but like Carlton said, you just run yourself ragged trying to support everyone. In my department, the squeaky wheel is always the group I end up spending the most time with, and then I don't get to the other groups.

Luis: Has anyone considered location and proximity? Or even having your entire content-group meeting in the same room? We do all have the same planning period now, which is pretty much unheard of in most high schools.

Tracie: That sounds like something I think my group could easily morph into next semester. We already begin our meetings together each week, and I share common announcements and such. A few times, two or three of the groups have just not relocated and instead stayed in the same room. It's been a gradual thing, but now it seems like most weeks the groups don't relocate. It saves them time, and they don't really get in one another's way in terms of different conversations going on at the same time. As the department chair, this has allowed me to monitor on a more consistent basis.

Luis: I like that it has evolved organically for your group, Tracie. What about other groups? Do you see this as something you can try to start the semester with? One common day of the week, beginning with announcements, celebrations, and possibly a mini-PD to share best practices, and then calendar work?

The group members agree to try this approach with their departments as the next semester begins. They also agree to blog each Friday about how it is going so the department chairs can continue to learn from one another's experiences.

The closing dialogue in this chapter demonstrates how leaders can center C.R.A.F.T. conversations on an individual cornerstone. Through thoughtful planning, Luis was able to focus the energy of his department chairs on building capacity. Take a moment to reflect on the last few conversations you had with different teachers or groups. What cornerstone was highlighted? The four cornerstones are designed to maximize the impact of your C.R.A.F.T. conversations.

Closing Thoughts

The four cornerstones provide the framework needed to make C.R.A.F.T. conversations powerful tools in your building. By starting with a focus on building capacity, you are creating a better school, working from the inside out. Change becomes palatable—some might even say exciting—as teachers share their new knowledge and begin to work collaboratively. Before you know it, there are many things to celebrate!

Understanding the components of C.R.A.F.T. conversations and the four cornerstones is vital. But how do you *really* have a C.R.A.F.T.

conversation? It starts with planning. Chapter 3 will lay out the skills and processes involved in crafting conversations. We also will offer our first set of cornerstone questions to guide you as we continue to examine the four cornerstones. In doing so, we hope to help you not only face some of the most challenging situations in your building but also develop your ability to make every conversation you engage in count.

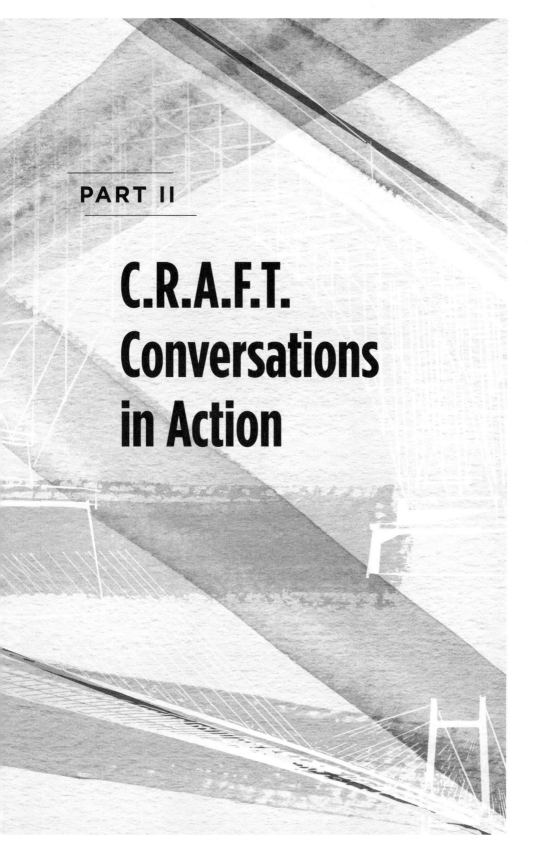

PART II

C.R.A.F.T. Conversations in Action

3 Planning for C.R.A.F.T. Conversations

Conversation is a meeting of minds with different memories and habits. When minds meet, they don't just exchange facts: they transform them, reshape them, draw different implications from them, engage in new trains of thought. Conversation doesn't just reshuffle the cards: it creates new cards.

—Theodore Zeldin,
Conversation: How Talk Can Change Our Lives (1998)

INSIDE THIS CHAPTER:

- Getting to Know Your Teachers
- Relationship Rules
- Keeping the End in Mind from the Beginning

Meera has been assigned to evaluate teachers in the social studies department during the coming school year. Of the 12 teachers she is responsible for, 8 are returning as social studies teachers from the previous year, and 2 are returning from the previous year but are new to the social studies department. The remaining 2 teachers are new to the school, and Meera really needs to get to know them on a more intimate level.

One of the new teachers, Michael, brings 12 years of experience with him from another district in the state. Meera is eager to learn more about his areas of expertise in order to position him as a leader in the department. She begins to plan for her first C.R.A.F.T. conversation with Michael to establish rapport and to learn more about his first week as a veteran teacher in a new building.

Schools are busy places, and C.R.A.F.T. conversations can take place at any time, with anyone, in any place. However, the key to making C.R.A.F.T. conversations count is being prepared. Prepared? That might seem like a challenging concept because of the organic nature of conversations. After all, it's hard to be prepared for the conversation that takes place when a teary-eyed teacher runs into your office just as the dismissal bell rings.

This chapter outlines how to prepare for C.R.A.F.T. conversations— a process that often begins long before preplanning and the first day of school. Remember that the foundation of planning for *all* C.R.A.F.T. conversations is the same. However, throughout the chapter we will provide you with cornerstone questions that will assist you when planning with a specific cornerstone in mind.

Getting to Know Your Teachers

We've all had that moment. You have just completed five interviews with prospective hires, and there is one more to go. The 2nd grade position is filled, but a dynamic teacher is needed to round out the 4th grade team. You quickly peruse the applicant's résumé. Undergraduate degree? Check. Valid teaching certificate? Check. Certification in gifted education? Check. The page reveals nothing outside of the ordinary, and all of the required boxes are checked.

The interview begins, and you are midway through your scripted questions when it happens. The interview turns into an honest and open conversation. You begin to find out more about what makes this teacher unique. You even share a few anecdotes from your own teaching career. As the interview closes, you know two things: (1) she's hired; and (2) you have a real sense of not only who she is as an educator but also who she is as a human being.

It's easy to talk about who our teachers are in the classroom. We have observed them teach numerous times. We have reviewed their lesson plans and interacted with them during team meetings, professional development sessions, and other situations. We can speak easily about their classroom practices, punctuality, and professionalism. But who are they really? Do we know our teachers on a personal level?

The first step in planning for C.R.A.F.T. conversations is to get to know your teachers. Think about some of the best conversations you have had. We have all had conversations that stirred our thoughts, shaped our path, and influenced our lives, and chances are that these conversations took place with someone we knew well. To unlock the power of C.R.A.F.T. conversations, you must be willing to put in the time, dedication, and effort that it takes to get to know your teachers.

So where do you begin? It is impossible to know everything about each one of your teachers. However, when it comes to C.R.A.F.T. conversations, some pieces of information are critical for success. Knowing certain information about teachers in the following areas can support your efforts to engage in C.R.A.F.T. conversations:

- Values and beliefs
- Mindset
- Career continuum placement
- Strengths and areas of opportunity
- Current classroom challenges and successes

Values and Beliefs

Every teacher is unique, and it is important to identify what makes them individuals. One way to begin is by gaining an understanding of what the teacher values and believes. Here are some questions to get you thinking about each teacher:

- Does family come first for this teacher?
- Is this teacher a proponent of standardized testing?
- Does this teacher value quality time or words of affirmation?
- How does this teacher feel about recent district mandates?

When you know more about what your teachers value and believe, you are able to get a glimpse of who they are as educators and individuals. You can then identify your differences and commonalities. You can also begin to internalize individual preferences that will be extremely beneficial when engaging in C.R.A.F.T. conversations. For example, if you know that Mrs. Rollins values quality time alone in the morning, you would avoid having important conversations with her while preparing morning coffee in the break room.

Mindset

Mindset speaks to an individual's attitude, way of thinking, or general disposition. Often our mindset heavily influences how we interpret situations and how we respond. Understanding a teacher's mindset is far more nuanced than understanding values and beliefs. A teacher's mindset cannot be fully revealed in answers to a series of questions but can be highlighted through repeated actions. In other words, pay attention to what your teachers say, but more important, pay attention to what your teachers *do* and how they respond to situations that arise.

What words does the teacher use when describing students who are challenging in the classroom? How does the teacher interact with parents? How often does the teacher engage with colleagues during professional development?

When you understand a teacher's mindset, you have a better understanding of the possible assumptions, biases, or baggage he or she might bring into the conversation. This understanding allows you to anticipate how teachers might act or respond during a conversation.

Career Continuum Placement

Part of what makes any school great is its teachers' wide range of experience. There are 25-year veteran teachers who have dedicated their lives to educating children, and recent college graduates who have been dreaming of their first day of school as real teachers. There are second-career teachers who recently said goodbye to the corporate world and are working through an alternative certification program. It is important to remember that everyone's journey to teaching is different, so everyone's knowledge and levels of expertise will vary as well. Everyone is at different points on the career continuum, and everyone brings something special to the table. However, leaders must have consistent expectations for exemplary instruction by all.

The *A* in C.R.A.F.T. emphasizes a leader's need to be *appropriate,* and this factor is particularly important when looking at the career continuum. The questions you pose to a veteran teacher might be vastly different from those you would ask a first-year teacher. The anecdotes you might share with someone who recently made a mid-career shift from being a banker to being a math teacher are probably not the same ones you would share with the third-year teacher who, like many others at this critical time, might be considering leaving the profession. As you prepare for conversations with your teachers, knowing where each teacher is on the continuum is crucial.

It is also vital to remember that teachers' place on the career continuum is not always dictated by their age. Although age is something to consider, the focus should be on the number of years spent in education. When you know how long teachers have been in the field, you have a deeper understanding of the various buzzwords they have seen come and go, some of the instructional strategies they have seen implemented, and the reform models and agendas that have shaped their experience. This information allows you to plan more carefully and intentionally.

Strengths and Areas of Opportunity

Leading an extraordinary school is similar to leading or coaching a championship team, where every player brings a unique skill set. It is up to the leader or coach to understand each player's strengths and to place each individual in the right position to give the team the best chance of winning. At the same time, great leaders and coaches realize that knowing their players' strengths is not enough. Knowledge of each player's areas of opportunity, or weaker points, must also be gained and used to help the overall team.

Imagine that you are gearing up for a winning season. What can you share about each of your teachers' strengths and areas of opportunity? Most of this knowledge comes from observations. As you visit classrooms, it becomes obvious who is a strong lesson planner, who has solid classroom management skills, and who is a whiz at differentiating instruction. Other observations that you make during morning routines, lunch duty, and even while attending after-school events can provide you with additional information about your teachers' skill sets. However, one-on-one conversations with your teachers can often reveal more information about strengths and areas of opportunity.

Have you ever taken the time to sit down with a teacher and simply ask, "What are your strengths?" or "What are some areas of opportunity that you would like to work on this year?" When having conferences before an observation, ask the teacher what area he thinks he could really strive to be exemplary in by the end of the school year. This question will set the tone and let the teacher know that you will be looking for the best in him and not always seeking to call attention to a weakness. These types of conversations should continue throughout the school year.

C.R.A.F.T. conversations have a much better chance of being successful when you know your teachers' strengths and areas of opportunity. Their strengths can be used as points of praise and leverage to help achieve school goals. Their areas of opportunity can help you determine how to approach certain issues and to keep the momentum going after the conversation by providing appropriate types of support. Try to avoid the word *weakness* in your conversations by focusing on opportunities that lead to growth and on your desire to add to each teacher's repertoire of strengths.

Current Classroom Challenges and Successes

Everyone has either worked for or heard of school leaders who can never be found. They are always out of the building at a district meeting or in their office completing paperwork. Their teachers voice age-old complaints such as "They have only been in my classroom once the entire year and it's February!" or "They only come when it's time for my evaluation, and I just perform the dog-and-pony show for the day." The job of a school leader is multifaceted, fast-paced, and at times overwhelming. It can be challenging for leaders to ensure that their presence is felt in their building and that teachers and students are accustomed to them being in classrooms throughout the school year—challenging, but not impossible!

Remember the *T* in C.R.A.F.T? It stands for *timely*. One of the most important things for a leader to do is to have current knowledge of what is happening in classrooms so that issues can be addressed in a prompt and productive fashion. Conversations in schools simply don't count or make a difference when leadership works with outdated knowledge and concerns. As the school year progresses, teachers experience different successes and challenges in the classroom. What they are having difficulty with in January might not be the same thing that sent them home in frustration in October. What they are patting themselves on the back for in March might be exactly what they were crying about in December. It's a leader's job to stay current. The question is, how?

A great way to stay current is to intentionally schedule your time so you can visit classrooms on a regular basis. If doing so means blocking out a few hours of time on your calendar as if you were attending a district meeting, do it.

Keep in mind that these visits should not always be tied to your teacher evaluation system. You should be visiting to learn more about what is happening in the classroom. Take the time to sit down with a group of students and engage in an activity. Take a moment to look around the room and see what type of student work is posted or which students are showing growth on the mastery tracker. Reflect on the teacher's actions, commentary, and tone. Don't always visit at the same time of the day. Vary your schedule so you can see classrooms at different times. One teacher may be nailing the morning routine but struggling when students return from lunch, finding it difficult to keep students engaged until the end of the school day.

You are probably thinking, "I don't have time to do all of this!" Although nothing can replace first-hand knowledge, you can also stay current by using a distributed leadership approach. Schedule one hour a week to meet with your instructional coaches to discuss what they are observing in classrooms. Request that your team leaders or grade-level chairs fill out a monthly survey that asks questions such as "What is your grade level most proud of this month?" or "What is the one challenge that your team plans to tackle next month, and how?" By making it a priority to know the challenges and successes teachers are experiencing in the classroom, you are continuously laying the foundation for successful C.R.A.F.T. conversations throughout the school year.

By involving others, school leaders enlarge the conversation base and can focus on developing capacity. But as they work to provide teachers with individualized and robust support by including others, such as fellow teachers, teacher leaders, and instructional and peer coaches, school leaders need to be cognizant of the importance of trust. The coaching literature suggests consensus on the point that the content of coaching conversations is, for the most part, sacred. We agree with the conventional thinking that coaching is a confidential process in which a teacher and a coach or a team of teachers and a coach work both independently and mutually on the development of instructional and classroom practices (Knight, 2011, 2017; Lofthouse, Leat, & Towler, 2010; Zepeda, 2015). However, coaches also work alongside school leaders to forward the instructional program, to support professional learning, and to engage teachers in learning how to work more effectively with students to improve achievement.

We agree that, as a rule, what occurs between a coach and a teacher should be confidential and must not become headline news among other teachers and school leaders. However, coaches, like other teacher leaders, regardless of role and function or job description, are on the front line in classrooms, at team and grade-level meetings, and during collaborative planning sessions, for example. As such, coaches have keen insights on what types of additional support teachers and programs need. These are insights that need to be shared with school leaders.

As with coaches, we believe that teacher leaders who engage in conversations can and should share information in ways that do not compromise relationships by over-identifying teachers or teams in ways that violate trust. This belief tells us that principals, assistant principals, and teacher leaders must balance the need to share information with care for individuals, and they must maintain trust when forwarding conversations that can make a difference in the lives of teachers and their schools.

Ways to Get to Know Your Teachers

Although there are many things to know and understand about your teachers, a focus on the areas just discussed—values and beliefs, mindset, career continuum placement, strengths and areas of opportunity, and current challenges and successes—is most effective when considering C.R.A.F.T. conversations. Remember, this process begins with your first interaction with a teacher and should continue throughout the school year. Here are a few formal and informal ways for you to get to know your teachers:

- Résumé
- Cover letter submitted with résumé and job application
- Sample teaching video
- LinkedIn profile
- Collaborative planning sessions
- Professional learning communities
- Conversations
- Classroom observations
- Surveys and questionnaires

As you begin to consider how well you know your teachers and what methods you already use to gather information, it should be evident how crucial planning is to a successful C.R.A.F.T. conversation. While planning, it is important to reflect on the four cornerstones of C.R.A.F.T. conversations and how one or more cornerstone is linked to the overall purpose of your conversation. Throughout this chapter and the next chapters, you will find sets of cornerstone questions to guide your reflection. These questions are not complex or verbose. They are designed to elicit thought related to your current situation while encouraging intention when connecting your conversations with one of the four cornerstones.

> **?**
>
> ## Cornerstone Questions: *Building Capacity*
>
> When planning for a C.R.A.F.T. conversation, it is pertinent to consider how you are supporting teachers and encouraging their development in an individualized manner. Here are questions to ponder as you plan for a C.R.A.F.T. conversation with a focus on getting to know your teachers and building capacity:
>
> - What are the teacher's current strengths and areas of opportunity?
> - What have you worked on with this teacher in the past (e.g., data analysis, parent communication)?
> - How does this teacher learn best (e.g., peer observation, watching a video, reading a book)?
> - Does this teacher have additional school duties and responsibilities outside of the norm (e.g., varsity softball coach, debate team coach)?
> - What is the one thing that this teacher could do differently that would have the greatest impact on student success?
>
> Taking time to think about individual teachers and their unique characteristics, such as learning styles, strengths, and additional school roles, can help you to determine the most effective and efficient path towards growth. Are there other cornerstone questions that come to mind that are specific to your school when you think about building capacity?

Relationship Rules

If you pick up any best-selling book on conversations, nine times out of ten you will find some commentary on relationships. Relationships are critical to productive and honest conversations. C.R.A.F.T. conversations are no different. If you want to make them count in your school, you must live by a simple mantra: *Relationships matter.*

Perhaps you have had a chance encounter with a total stranger that left you with a memorable experience and a few pearls of wisdom. You're at the airport gate waiting for your plane, which is delayed for two hours, when the woman next to you strikes up a conversation, and before you know it, the time has flown by! It happens! However, most fruitful conversations take place with someone you have a solid relationship with, whether you are colleagues or best friends.

The word *relationship* often seems like one of those "warm and fuzzy" words. For some school leaders, the term immediately blurs the boundary between personal and professional. When it comes to C.R.A.F.T. conversations, relationships are based on understanding what connects you to your teachers. In other words, how are you and your teachers related? At the most basic level, you work at the same school. That's at least a starting point. However, to begin to build quality relationships with your teachers, it is important to uncover more connections. This does not mean sharing your deepest secrets. It means engaging in ordinary conversations and simply paying attention. Quality relationships are the foundation of C.R.A.F.T. conversations that count. In the following sections we discuss things to consider in your effort to build quality relationships.

Claim Your Baggage

When you claim your baggage, you own *your* personal strengths and weaknesses. It is easy to view relationships in a one-sided manner. We often think *only* about what the teacher is bringing to the table. But what about the leader? Here are some questions to get you thinking:

- What funds of knowledge are *you* bringing to the table?
- What are *you* currently working on as a professional?
- What about *your* work history or experience could cloud the conversation?
- How do *you* typically react when conversations become extremely tense or uncomfortable?
- What's *your* history with this teacher?

As the leader, you are already positioned in a seat of power before the conversation begins, like it or not. By being reflective and transparent about who you are and what you bring to the table, you are in many ways leveling the playing field and setting the stage for a conversation in which titles do not play such a hefty role.

Consider Your Relationship Status

Your relationships with teachers will vary from day to day and from year to year. Perhaps you have known the lead of your 3rd grade team since you were kids. You both went to the same high school and never lost touch after graduation. Your sons even play on the same baseball team. Your relationship with this teacher is probably solid. On the other hand, you've known your literacy coach for 16 years. You both became teachers in the district at the same time and were even promoted to be instructional coaches in the same cluster. Five years ago, you both applied for the principalship at your school. You got the job. When the district transferred her to your school two years ago, the tension was more than obvious. Needless to say, your relationship with this colleague probably leaves much to be desired.

The first rule of thumb is to be honest with yourself. Do you have a good relationship with the teacher you are meeting with, or is it strained? If it is strained, is it beyond repair? If you don't have a relationship with the teacher at all, why not? It can be so much easier to ignore reality or to place the blame on someone else when answering these questions. You might tell yourself, "Our relationship is not *that* bad," or "We had an awesome relationship until she decided to hold a grudge when she wasn't named Teacher of the Year." It is this type of thinking that can make conversations difficult and uncomfortable.

It is important to reflect on your own actions and to determine what you have done that has led to a successful relationship or to one that needs to be resuscitated. It is also worth noting that some relationships will never be what you desire, no matter what you do. That's OK. Relationships occur between human beings, and that means some things will be out of your control. Telling yourself the truth, however, is not out of your control.

Understand That Continuous Work Is Required

Relationships require work. As a school leader, it is critical to understand that part of your work is building and sustaining relationships with your teachers. Most people are already familiar with how to *build* a relationship. It begins with many of the things that have already been discussed, such as honesty, commonalities, and communication. *Sustaining* a relationship is what often proves to be most challenging.

Sustaining a relationship takes two things: commitment and time. By now you should realize the value that quality relationships can bring not only to your C.R.A.F.T. conversations but also to the success of your school as a whole. When things are of value, it is usually easier to commit and give them the time and energy they require. Being committed to sustaining your relationships with teachers is a continuous and constant exercise in your ability to connect with people in an effort to understand, empathize, and support. You have to be curious and concerned. You have to engage, discuss, and observe. If you are willing to commit and to use your time wisely, the payoff is huge. In schools where C.R.A.F.T. conversations count, leaders are working every day to ensure that relationships are being either formed or fortified.

Cornerstone Questions: *Invoking Change*

This set of cornerstone questions is designed to provoke thought connected to planning for change. Similar to relationships, change does not take place without commitment and time. For change to occur, school leaders must understand that teachers are the primary catalysts. Consider these questions as you prepare to meet with teachers when invoking change is on the horizon:

- What is the teacher's current context (i.e., the teacher's classroom)?
- Are there any mindsets that might prevent this teacher from moving forward with change?
- How is this teacher typically motivated?
- How does this teacher usually respond to change?
- What has helped this teacher try or succeed with changes in the past (e.g., workshop, data)?

Some teachers and leaders view change as negative or something that is hard to achieve. Change is not negative, and it certainly does not have to be arduous. The key to invoking change is to set teachers up for maximum success by preparing with them in mind. When you know how your teachers typically respond to change or what motivates them, you might find yourself adjusting your approach to make it more cohesive and successful.

Keep It Professional

Is the word *relationship* still a bit too warm and fuzzy for you? We hope not, but if so, rest assured that C.R.A.F.T. conversations in schools require relationships that are professional. Like personal relationships, professional relationships are marked by certain key characteristics, such as honesty, open communication, and trust. However, they tend not to require teachers to reveal their innermost thoughts, share their secrets, or reveal all the skeletons in their closets. So how does a school leader keep it professional?

First, ensure that your C.R.A.F.T. conversations are grounded in what school is all about—the kids. C.R.A.F.T. conversations are always steeped in matters that speak to the overall well-being of the children you serve. Whether the discussion is about grading practices, classroom culture, or a parent concern, always enter into the conversation knowing that the result should benefit children. By putting your students first, you are less likely to be sidetracked and veer into personal territory.

Second, do not attempt to have an "Oprah moment." We've all watched Oprah in action. She looks deeply into her guests' eyes and asks hard-hitting questions that make people examine their heart and soul. She gets into the gritty details of the past. Well, you are a school leader, not Oprah! Sure, you've probably had moments when you had to hand a teacher a box of tissues to wipe away tears, or maybe you've even had conversations in which teachers voluntarily share that their pet passed away or that they are going through a tough divorce. That's not a bad thing, and to be honest, conversations of that type are hard to avoid when you are someone's boss. However, do not go digging for details. Show that you care, but remember you are a school leader, not a licensed therapist.

Remember That Differentiation Is Not Just for the Classroom

The word *differentiation* excites some and scares many. It frightens some teachers because they either do not understand what differentiation means in its most simplistic form or because they do not fully understand the amount of time and work required to do it well. Regardless, quality teachers and leaders alike know that a one-size-fits-all approach doesn't work for students. It doesn't work for teachers either.

If you want to make C.R.A.F.T. conversations count in your school, be sure to maintain a focus on the *R* and be *realistic*. Customization and individualization are key as you focus on each teacher and his or her unique set of circumstances. Different teachers need different things at different times. To differentiate in a C.R.A.F.T. conversation, you have to carefully combine your knowledge of the teacher with your understanding of the status of the relationship the two of you share. In doing so, you are able to answer questions such as these:

- What are this teacher's interests?
- What is this teacher ready to hear?
- What approach would be best for delivering this critical feedback?

Being able to answer these questions enables you to create a tailor-made experience within the conversation. By individualizing your approach, you are maximizing your opportunity to help the teacher grow and evolve.

Remember the Mantra

Do you remember our mantra? *Relationships matter!* So make sure you consider the relationship rules we've just discussed. Claim your baggage and always be honest with yourself about where your relationships with teachers stand. Commit to the continuous work that is required to build and sustain your relationships, and always keep it professional and as tailor-made as possible. Doing so allows you to keep the foundation for your C.R.A.F.T. conversations fertile and alive.

Cornerstone Questions: *Promoting Collaboration*

The following cornerstone questions are designed to remind you that relationships are valuable throughout your building and are key when trying to establish a culture of collaboration. Although it is important for leaders to take time to collaborate with teachers, it is even more valuable when colleagues see collaboration as a way of life that enhances everything they do. As you plan for C.R.A.F.T. conversations, keep collaboration at the forefront of your mind by considering questions such as these:

- How does this teacher use the time currently allotted for collaboration?
- What are this teacher's favorite ways to collaborate (e.g., brainstorming session, Google Docs)?
- When working in a group, what role does this teacher typically play?
- What best practices have you seen in this teacher's classroom that would most benefit other teachers and students?
- What is this teacher's biggest passion when it comes to teaching and learning?

How do you currently promote collaboration in your building? Maybe when you read through this set of cornerstone questions you realized that teachers at your school mostly work in silos. Maybe your school has set up the constructs for collaboration, but you are not clear on how or if they function. Through careful planning, you can use these questions to begin to build your own set of guiding principles to effectively promote collaboration in your building.

Keeping the End in Mind from the Beginning

Every conversation has a purpose. Some are needed to express a concern, whereas others take place to make others laugh or brighten their day. Many conversations occur as a way for individuals to exchange ideas, plan, or collaborate, and some are just everyday exchanges to express greetings or say goodbye. Whether planned, routine, or spontaneous, every conversation has a basis and a motive that drives it forward. To ensure your C.R.A.F.T. conversations count, it is important to be aware of the purpose of your conversation and to establish goals and outcomes early.

Remember That Purpose Is Paramount

The purpose of the conversation speaks to the reason why the conversation is taking place. In most cases, leaders are already acutely aware of the purpose because it is exactly what has prompted them to schedule the meeting in the first place. However, sometimes teachers approach leaders to have an impromptu conversation. Leaders might not know the purpose, but it is critical to hone in on it as the conversation unfolds, and to do so as quickly as possible.

When you ask to meet with a teacher, your purpose should already be established. As the *C* in C.R.A.F.T. reminds us, it is important to be *clear*. In setting a clear purpose, you are allowing yourself adequate time to reflect and prepare for a C.R.A.F.T. conversation that will be specific and meaningful. If your purpose has not been established, you will be entering the conversation blindly and can easily get lost or sidetracked, resulting in a conversation that leaves both parties more confused or perhaps more dissatisfied than before. If you can't establish a purpose, ask yourself, "Is this conversation necessary?" or "Why do I need to have a one-on-one conversation with this teacher?"

It is also important to share your purpose with the teacher when appropriate. We all remember, in our early years of teaching, that gut-wrenching sensation that came right after our principal said, "We need to talk," or the agonizing moment when we saw an e-mail from our principal titled "Meeting Request." For many teachers, the idea of having a conversation with leadership causes anxiety, even when leaders have established a school culture that includes conversations as an integral part.

You cannot control a teacher's reaction, but you can provide information that will establish understanding and clarity. By sharing the purpose of the conversation with the teacher, you are setting the stage for an effective C.R.A.F.T. conversation in which both individuals know the purpose and can prepare appropriately.

So what about the conversations that are not initiated by you? Often teachers will approach leaders and simply ask, "Do you have a moment?" Some will send an e-mail requesting a time to meet. It is still vital for you to know why this person wants to meet. Often leaders make assumptions. They think to themselves, "I know this teacher wants to meet with me about her tardiness because she turned red when I saw her sign in late last Friday." Making assumptions is a dangerous practice. Never assume. If a teacher requests a meeting, always ask for clarity around the purpose. Even if the conversation is spontaneous, it is still appropriate to ask a question such as "What would you like to discuss?" The answer can help you determine the right location for the conversation, and in some instances, it can help you make an informed decision that the current time is not suitable.

Establish Your Goals and Desired Outcomes Early

Solidifying goals and outcomes can often be challenging. Sometimes so many things need improvement that it becomes cumbersome for you to choose just one. Other times you might have a goal or an outcome in mind, but you are not sure if it's the right one because of the teacher's current classroom challenges or even the time of year. Regardless, it takes time and effort to develop a goal that is appropriate and worthy of action. When planning, ask yourself questions such as "What exactly do I hope to gain from the conversation?" or "What do I want or need to happen as a result of having the conversation?"

When your aim is clear, you can plan your questions and draft a general flow for the conversation. For example, if you know that the goal of your conversation with Ms. Lindsay is to ensure that she understands and can use the school's lesson plan framework, you might start the conversation by asking, "How do you approach lesson planning?" or "Tell me about the process you use to start developing your lesson plan." You also might have a few of her lesson plans printed out, as well as a few exemplars from other teachers to share. It is important to refer back to the *F* in C.R.A.F.T., which stands for *flexible*. As you engage with the teacher, you might find that your goal needs to be tweaked or your questions need to go in a slightly different direction based on some of her responses. It is perfectly fine to adjust in the moment.

By establishing your goals and outcomes in advance, you are also reinforcing the importance of action. C.R.A.F.T. conversations never take place "just because." C.R.A.F.T. conversations have a purpose and are always marked by action. In other words, when the conversation has come to a close, the teacher and the leader must do certain things. These actions are driven by the goals and outcomes of the conversation. That's why it is crucial to know your target before the conversation begins.

? Cornerstone Questions: *Prioritizing Celebration*

This set of cornerstone questions is designed to remind you to plan for the positive. Although setting goals is a standard leadership practice, too often, celebration seems to be an afterthought. When teachers achieve their goals or perform exceptionally in the classroom, they should be celebrated. If you focus on celebration when planning your C.R.A.F.T. conversations, it will soon become part of your routine practice. Use these questions to get started on this aspect of planning:

- How does this teacher like to be celebrated?
- When was the last time this teacher was celebrated?
- What has this teacher been celebrated for in the past?
- How have you seen this teacher celebrate others in the past?
- What is this teacher doing well?

As you reflect on this set of cornerstone questions, you may be alarmed at the lack of celebration in your building. It's definitely one of those things that can easily be forgotten, as leaders tend to always focus on the next hurdle or challenge. By prioritizing celebration, you are making a clear statement that great work deserves to be acknowledged and it is OK to raise a glass now, before moving full force into the future.

Let's revisit the vignette from the beginning of the chapter. Remember, this chapter is all about planning and getting to know your teachers. Meera's primary focus is to build a positive rapport with Michael. She also wants to draw upon the expertise he brings as she promotes teacher leadership in the social studies department.

Meera: Thanks for meeting with me today. Tell me how your first week went, Michael.

Michael: Oh, it was great! The teachers here are so nice, and the kids are great too!

Meera: Do you feel like you have everything you need to start out the year strong?

Michael: Well, not all of my students were able to bring supplies. What do I do about that?

Meera: We have a supply closet that I can take you to when we finish so you can see if there are items you need.

Michael: Oh, that would be great. Thanks so much!

Meera: Well, I'm glad your year has gotten off to a good start. I know we covered your experience in your interview, but I'd like to go a bit deeper and learn more about you. Could you tell me a little bit more about your experience and how your path in education has led you to us?

Michael: I have 12 years of experience in another district in the state. I taught 8th grade Georgia history for most of that time, and the last four years I was the social studies department chair.

Meera: Well, we're lucky to have you here. I can tell you bring a wealth of knowledge that will keep our school moving forward in a positive direction. What else can you tell me that can help me get to know a little more about your journey as an educator?

Michael: I want you to know that I really feel at home here. I went to a school very similar to this one. My mom and my dad worked several jobs to make sure we had the best possible situation as far as our education went. It was a blessing growing up in Georgia because I was able to fund my college education through the HOPE Grant. My family is large and we're very close, and my grandmother still lives with my folks. My sister is studying to be a counselor right now at the local state college because she really wants to help kids like we were. The school played a vital role in my career path, and I really just want to give back. I love to set the path for my kids and the teachers I work with too.

Meera: Thank you for sharing your story with me, Michael. I know your experiences will bring a great deal of positivity to our school, and it sounds like you are up for a leadership role right off the bat.

Michael: Yes, of course. Whatever I can do to help, in any way, is what I want to do!

Meera: Keep me informed about your sister as she progresses through her studies. It would be great to have a brother-and-sister team here.

Michael: Of course! I know she'll be happy to hear that, and I'll make sure she comes to meet you during her fall break this year.

Meera: That would be perfect! Now, I don't want to keep you too long. I wanted to make sure you're familiar with the 10 standards in our state evaluation system.

Michael: Yes—they're the same ones we used where I came from.

Meera: So if you were to pick one or two of those standards that you would really like to shoot for in terms of an exemplary rating for this year, which would you pick?

Michael: Well, definitely the "Differentiation" standard. I'm really good at analyzing data and using it for grouping in my classroom to make sure the kids are getting what they need to be successful.

Meera: I noticed that you had your students grouped when I stopped by at the beginning of the week for a visit, but I wasn't sure if it was purposeful.

Michael: Oh, everything I do in my classroom is purposeful! The pre-test data from the second day of school gave me a place to start. Now I'm assessing students daily with an exit ticket as they leave the classroom so I can see how the groups need to be established from day to day. My kids have to get used to change right from the get-go. Nothing stays the same in my classroom from one day to the next.

Meera: Great! So how do you think the way you use differentiation in your classroom can serve as a model to your peers? That's the piece that sets an exemplary rating apart from a proficient one.

Michael: One way I do that is during common planning meetings. I make sure I share the formative assessment practices I'm using to assess and group my students pretty much on a daily basis. I also use stations a good bit, and I level them and then group my students according to my daily assessment. Another way I model for my peers is by opening up my classroom. My room is always open for observations if needed.

Meera: We do a good bit of peer-to-peer as well as group lesson studies here, so I'll definitely remember that when it comes time to plan those visits. I'll count on you to lead in that area, and I look forward to follow-up conversations about differentiation. What is another area you would like to focus on this year as a stand-out?

Michael: Probably "Academically Challenging" and "Instructional Planning." I work hard to keep my classroom instruction engaging and efficient. There is no time wasted, and I dare a student to tell me he or she is bored!

Meera: I really look forward to this year with you, Michael. I can already see that I have a lot to learn from you and that you bring so much to the table. Don't forget to keep me up to date on your sister's progress in school. It sounds like we have an exciting year in store. Please plan to talk about differentiation at our first curriculum meeting next Wednesday—just a brief example, no more than three or four minutes. Feel free to bring artifacts you use if you would like to, but it really isn't necessary. Our first meeting will focus on the 10 standards, and 10 different teachers will present a short example to invoke thought as they plan to meet and exceed a particular standard throughout the school year.

Michael: I'm so happy to be here and really look forward to the collaboration that I can already see throughout the school. I look forward to stepping up and helping wherever I can this year.

Meera: We are so lucky to have you, Michael! I'll see you at some point tomorrow in my daily classroom-cruise time.

This C.R.A.F.T. conversation focuses on getting to know your teachers and garnering a better understanding of their mindsets and goals. Meera was able to gather additional information about Michael that helped her to learn more about what he brought to the table. The conversation opened the door for Michael to share as much or as little about himself as he wanted. By asking the teacher to share his thoughts about his strengths, Meera was able to set a positive tone while still gathering key information.

Closing Thoughts

As this chapter has illustrated, planning for C.R.A.F.T. conversations is hard work. It involves getting to know your teachers, understanding relationship rules, and keeping the end in mind from the beginning of every conversation. Some of these steps can be worked on daily, whereas others will require more focused energy and time. If you want your C.R.A.F.T. conversations to count, you must commit to the planning phase 100 percent. Once you have planned for a C.R.A.F.T. conversation, it is time for the main event—the conversation itself!

Take some time to go back through this chapter and reflect on each set of cornerstone questions and to think about which pieces of the planning phase you excel in already and which components you need to give more time and attention to in order to move conversations forward. In Chapter 4, you will learn more about the engagement portion of a C.R.A.F.T. conversation and how to make sure that both parties are active participants.

4

Engaging in C.R.A.F.T. Conversations

Sometimes you have to disconnect to stay connected. Remember the old days when you had eye contact during a conversation? When everyone wasn't looking down at a device in their hands? We've become so focused on that tiny screen that we forget the big picture, the people right in front of us.

—Regina Brett, American journalist

INSIDE THIS CHAPTER:

The Core Four—
- Listening
- Inquiry
- Indicators
- Expertise

Lisa has been teaching at Brookfield Middle School for 18 years and has seen five principals come and go. She was granted tenure during a period when little to no documentation of performance was recorded. As a result, she was passed along from one leadership team to the next.

Rashad has been assigned as Lisa's evaluator for the year, and right off the bat he has concerns—even before setting foot in her classroom. Testing data reveals that most of Lisa's students have not met the "Satisfactory" level on standards on the state-mandated test over the past two years. Even though all students must take the state assessment, the grade level she teaches does not require students to pass the test for promotion purposes; promotion requires only that they take and pass certain classes. This situation has left an easy place for Lisa to hide, because all of her students consistently earn an *A* or a *B* in her class.

Rashad begins planning for his first C.R.A.F.T. conversation with Lisa. The area of concern is the level of her instruction. He gathers trend data from the state assessments not only for Lisa, but also for all the math teachers at her grade level. He also visits gradebook archives to see if final grades for students match their standardized test scores. Next, he schedules some time to visit her classroom for a few walkthroughs at various times of the day. Rashad wants to get a feel for her approach to differentiation and start to identify instructional strategies that are evident in her day-to-day instruction.

In Chapter 1, you were introduced to the key components of a C.R.A.F.T. conversation: planning, opening, engaging, closing, reflecting, and following up. As you learned, planning takes quite a bit of work and endurance. However, if you plan well, you are setting the stage for a positive opening that promotes engagement. Although the opening of the conversation sets the tone and outlines the purpose, the engagement component is the heart and soul of any C.R.A.F.T. conversation. This is where it happens!

When you think about engagement related to a conversation, your mind may immediately go to a back-and-forth exchange of ideas or a lot of talking on your part while the teacher listens and carefully takes notes. Although some of this certainly takes place during conversations, C.R.A.F.T. conversations require much more. Engagement happens at a deeper and more significant level centered on what we call the Core Four: Listening, Inquiry, Indicators, and Expertise. By examining these four elements of engagement, you will begin to understand their individual meaning and merit. The presence of all four increases the likelihood of engagement, leading to progress, innovation, and improvement.

The Core Four: Keys to Unlocking the Potential of C.R.A.F.T. Conversations

Imagine that you have spent some time planning for a C.R.A.F.T. conversation. You are feeling confident but also a bit anxious as you take a seat at the table with one of your science teachers. As you open the conversation, it is evident that the teacher is excited to engage with you. The tone is upbeat and supportive from the very beginning, which helps ease your nerves a bit. Then it's time to dig in! But what exactly does "digging in" look like?

When it's time to get to the nitty-gritty, the Core Four—Listening, Inquiry, Indicators, and Expertise—are critical (see Figure 4.1). They are the defining elements of the engagement component of a C.R.A.F.T.

FIGURE 4.1

The Core Four of C.R.A.F.T. Conversations

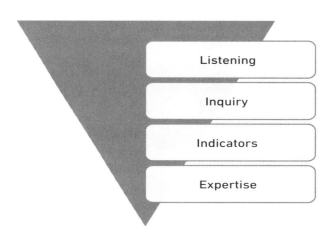

conversation. The Core Four help to elevate conversation from traditional discourse to an opportunity for growth and development for teachers. When all four of these elements are used skillfully, the conversation is authentic, collaborative, and often transformative.

It is important to note that the Core Four are listed in order of importance. In other words, Listening is your top priority in a C.R.A.F.T. conversation. Inquiry and Indicators are next, and Expertise is last. You might be shocked that Expertise is last on the list—and at the bottom of the triangle shown in Figure 4.1. Remember, you are partnering with your teachers to help them sharpen their skills. When you offer your expertise only when absolutely necessary, you leave ample space and opportunity for teachers to think critically and solve problems for themselves.

Listening

As educators, we spend a great deal of time doing most of the talking. C.R.A.F.T. conversations call for us to focus on listening. But what does listening entail? You probably think that you are a great listener, but would others say the same? For engagement to occur, listening must be thought of as a dynamic process, with constant change and activity occurring as conversations unfold.

For many of us, when we hear the term *conversation*, we immediately start to think about what we are going to say. Next, we might consider our tone, facial expressions, or overall body language. This is a natural process, because it's easy to focus on ourselves as we ponder how our message will be received.

What if we flipped this notion on its head and focused on what we *hear?* Check out any recent educational blog about engaging qualities of school leaders, and at the top of the list you will likely find something about being a good communicator. The most important component of communication is listening. This concept might seem foreign, but it is the art of listening that can often make or break a conversation.

C.R.A.F.T. conversations focus not just on listening, but more specifically on *actively* listening. When you actively listen, you let go of the urge to advise or counsel. You let go of the need to be ready to respond as soon as the teacher pauses or completes a thought. Instead, your focus is on being a full participant who seeks to understand the teacher's viewpoint. Active listening bolsters relationships, displays a high level of commitment, and places collaboration front and center.

When you are actively listening, your goal is to ensure understanding. You want the teacher to know that not only is his or her message being heard, but it is also clear and comprehensible. To listen actively, you must focus on the teacher's words and channel your energy into showing genuine interest through your body language and thoughtful responses. Let's think about what active listening could look like on a random Monday morning at work.

It may begin with a simple question, such as "How was your weekend?" It's so easy to zone out and wait for the teacher to finish and ask you about your own weekend. However, if you are actively listening, you are solely focused on the teacher. You are concentrating on words, intonation, and important details. When you have been actively listening and a natural pause occurs, you will likely have some follow-up questions to gain even more clarity. You may ask, "You said you've never seen your daughter so excited. What about the carnival got her going?" or "When you got to the dog park, how did you react when he jumped out of the car?" These kinds of questions show the teacher that you were listening to the details shared and that you are interested in hearing even more. It also gives the teacher latitude to tell you as little or as much as he or she would like. Although C.R.A.F.T. conversations might not begin with a simple question such as "How was your weekend?", the elements of active listening are still the same.

There are also myriad factors to consider to ensure that you are in the right frame of mind to fully concentrate on what is being said. Active listening isn't just staying silent and nodding your head to show interest. It's listening without judgment and with a desire to support the other person. You need to be prepared to offer thoughtful responses that continue to help the conversation evolve. For instance, if Sarah is telling you about a lesson she tried in which students had to work in pairs and it went horribly wrong, it is important for you to listen without judgment. Don't jump in and tell her how you would have done it or inform her that it was obvious that her students hadn't been taught the rules of collaboration. Remember that expertise is at the bottom of the Core Four triangle shown in Figure 4.1.

Instead, ask for further details about what she had hoped to see or what she would like to see in the future. The objective is to prompt the teacher to share more about her experience so that she can begin to uncover where things went awry. Let things flow organically. If Sarah asks for suggestions, be sparing and concentrate on probing for additional details from her, saying, for example, "You said the students were working in pairs. What are the rules in your classroom when students are working in pairs?" Continue to listen as Sarah reflects on her rules and provides you with more information to better understand her situation.

Full awareness is also a critical component of listening. Are you trying to multitask while listening? Are you seated behind your desk or at the far end of a gigantic conference table? What are you communicating through your body language? First, remember to focus on one thing—the actual conversation. This is not the time to try to listen while typing up your agenda for tomorrow's faculty meeting or quickly checking e-mail. Second, location matters. You should consider using a location that allows you and the teacher to sit side by side or perhaps at a round table so you can turn and make eye contact easily or offer a kind pat on the shoulder if and when appropriate. Third, keep in mind that your body language can often be the loudest statement in the room. Be mindful of what you are saying nonverbally. Your body language should show that you are engaged and ready to work alongside the teacher toward a common goal.

Body language can make or break a conversation. Craddick (2017) states that "the outcome of a conversation can vary greatly depending on the type of body language you're using" (para. 6). Essentially, body language is a type of nonverbal communication. You have heard the expressions "wearing your heart on your sleeve" and "having a poker face." Both of these evoke images of body language—one open (emotions on sleeves equals easy to read) and one closed (poker face equals difficult to read). Both examples illustrate that many messages are sent through nonverbal communication, including facial expressions. Lunenburg (2010) reminds us that "nonverbal communication—the way we stand, the distance we maintain from another person, the way we walk, the way we fold our arms and wrinkle our brow, our eye contact, being late for a meeting—conveys messages to others" (p. 1). Seminal studies in the late 1960s and early 1970s led to the "7%-38%-55% rule" (Mehrabian, 1971) in relation to credibility and communication. According to the rule, 7 percent of credibility is built on the content of what a person says, 38 percent is built on nonverbal cues (e.g., tone of voice), and 55 percent is built on facial expressions, gestures, and other body language. Figure 4.2 lists examples of body language and nonverbal cues that can derail a C.R.A.F.T. conversation.

FIGURE 4.2

**Types of Body Language and Nonverbal Cues
That Can Derail C.R.A.F.T. Conversations**

Types of Body Language	Nonverbal Cues
Eyes	Rolling eyes; squinting; sidewise glancing to avoid making eye contact with the person speaking; eyes on a screen (checking cell phones, texting, surfing the internet, answering e-mails, playing games online, etc.); covering eyes; not making eye contact or looking beyond the speaker at objects in the room
Hands	Finger pointing; tapping fingers on table; cracking knuckles
Arms	Arms folded; elbows on the table; hyperextended arms with clenched fists
Mouth	Scowling; baring/gritting teeth; tightening lips; yawning
Other	Tapping feet; shrugging shoulders; fidgeting; doodling and drawing; taking excessive notes

?

Cornerstone Questions: *Building Capacity*

This set of cornerstone questions centers on building capacity as it relates to the Core Four—specifically, Listening and Inquiry. Leaders can learn a lot about teachers by actively listening and probing throughout C.R.A.F.T. conversations. One of the best ways to begin to build capacity is by discovering teachers' own thoughts about their performance and skill level. You can use the following questions to guide the process:

- What does this teacher identify as personal strengths and areas of opportunity?
- Can the teacher articulate or identify steps he or she has taken to grow and develop?
- What has been unearthed during the conversation that is counterproductive to building capacity in the chosen area?
- How can inquiry be used during the conversation to skillfully build upon the teacher's existing knowledge base?
- Where are the gaps in the teacher's current understanding that need to be closed to move forward?

Listening to your teachers will make clear what they believe they know and are able to do. Although their thoughts may or may not align with what you have observed, building capacity starts with meeting teachers where they are, understanding their individual perceptions, and asking questions to begin to close any gaps.

Inquiry

Have you ever hung out with a toddler? They are loads of fun and laughter—until they start to ask, "Why?" "Well, why?" and "Why?" again! Toddlers are very inquisitive because so much of the world is new to them. They have a strong desire to understand what they see, hear, and experience in their day-to-day lives. When they begin to ask questions and those questions are answered honestly, the growth and development that follow are monumental. C.R.A.F.T. conversations are no different.

In C.R.A.F.T. conversations, it is important to approach things with fresh eyes. You are on a mission to discover and uncover, which means you have to ask questions. Inquiry is the act of seeking information. It provides a pathway toward understanding your teachers and their actions at a deeper level. The *R* in C.R.A.F.T. reminds us to be *realistic.* It may seem like the questions you ask are no-brainers, but remember that everyone perceives things differently, and understanding is easily represented on a sliding scale that can change by the day or the hour.

When you ask questions, you are stepping away from making assumptions and looking to gain first-hand knowledge into a teacher's thought process. Inquiry allows teachers to be the experts on their own personal experiences, and it shows that you are interested, open, and willing to listen.

Inquiry during a C.R.A.F.T. conversation is paramount. It takes careful thought and consideration to ensure that the right questions are being asked at the right time. However, the *F* in C.R.A.F.T. emphasizes the importance of being *flexible.* Although you might enter into a conversation thinking you know all of the necessary information or even having a variety of exemplars to share, the art of inquiry allows you to remain open-minded. Inquiry also allows you to go with the flow and follow the organic course of conversations while giving you an opportunity to hear the voice of the teacher.

As you begin to craft the questions you will ask, make sure that most of them are open-ended. Unlike closed-ended questions, open-ended questions cannot be answered with a simple yes or no. Consider these two questions:

1. Do you think that your e-mails to parents are professional?
2. What are some things you think about when composing e-mails to parents?

Question 1 is an example of a closed-ended question. The answer is yes or no. Question 2 is an open-ended question and allows for a more in-depth explanation. Both questions are valid, but the latter can provide more insight to help pinpoint the teacher's challenge.

You also want to make sure the questions you ask are not leading questions. Leading questions tend to make assumptions and are usually judgment laden. Here are two examples of leading questions:

1. When did you start to realize that your tardiness in coming to work was creating problems on your team?

2. How are you planning to work with Joshua so that he spends more time in your class than in the front office?

Both questions make assumptions. In Question 1, you are assuming that the teacher knows that she is creating problems for her team and that she realizes her tardiness is an issue. In Question 2, you are assuming that the teacher plans to work with Joshua. It is challenging not to ask a few leading questions, but try to refrain as much as possible. Also, make sure questions are focused to guide the conversation toward a specific outcome.

Once you have developed your questions, it is time to think about when to ask certain ones. Every conversation is different, and you can never plan for everything that may happen. However, your questions should follow a natural order. As an analogy, think about when you are meeting someone for the first time. You typically would ask, "What is your name?" before you ask a question such as "What do you like to do in your free time?"

Your questions should build on one another and help your teachers to think critically. Remember, your questions are just a guide. Once the conversation begins, be open and flexible. Don't feel pressured to ask every question in a lock-step order or to ask each one exactly as written. In fact, if you do, your conversation will probably feel sterile and be less effective than you desire.

Probing is another key factor when focusing on inquiry. However, it is a bit more challenging to plan. When you probe, you are asking follow-up questions based on the teacher's response. These questions are usually needed to help you better understand a response or to go deeper. Sometimes you might even probe to gather more specific information. Although probing is often overlooked, it can lead to increased growth in teachers because it encourages them to stretch their thinking in order to reflect, analyze, and actively problem-solve.

Let's look at how probing might play out in a C.R.A.F.T. conversation. You have planned to meet with a teacher who is having difficulty implementing the school's Positive Behavioral Intervention and Supports (PBIS) program. You plan to ask the following question first: "What is your current understanding of our school's PBIS program?" Although you have no way of knowing exactly how the teacher will respond, here are some possible probes:

• Tell me about a time when your use of PBIS had a positive effect on your classroom.

• What are some of the reasons you like/dislike PBIS?

Questions like these serve a larger purpose. In this case, although schoolwide change is often viewed at the macro level, it is the small individualized changes at the micro level that allow school change to occur.

Cornerstone Questions: *Invoking Change*

The following cornerstone questions can guide your thoughts as you consider a situation you may be facing with a teacher who is not fully committed to a program change:

• Has the teacher self-identified what needs to be altered or changed?

• How can you support the teacher in uncovering what needs to be changed and why?

• How long will it take for the desired change to occur, and what types of supports will the teacher need?

• How will you know when the change has become an embedded part of the teacher's practice?

• Does the teacher understand how the proposed change will positively affect students?

These cornerstone questions all have an individualized focus. During C.R.A.F.T. conversations, it is critical to approach change from a personalized point of view. Teachers may understand why a change is warranted overall, but it helps if they can speak to the importance of their unique role in making the change a reality.

Indicators

Do you remember one of the first science experiments you ever conducted? Perhaps there were two beakers in front of you, each with a different solution. You pulled on your latex gloves and felt like a true scientist as you picked up your strips of litmus paper and dipped one into each beaker. If the paper strip turned blue, that meant a base was present. If the paper turned red, acid was present. The litmus paper was an indicator of what was present in your solution. When we think of C.R.A.F.T. conversations, the indicators should work in the same fashion. Indicators should provide clear information on the state or condition of a teacher's classroom, pedagogy, parental contact, and everything in between.

An indicator is similar to a gauge or a measure. It provides straightforward information on the state or condition of something specific. When you schedule a conversation, something needs to be discussed. Whether it's parent communication, lack of active monitoring on the playground, or fair grading practices, every conversation typically has a focus. In a C.R.A.F.T. conversation, recall that the C stands for *clear*. This point is extremely important to remember when selecting indicators. Every indicator you use should paint a clear picture for the teacher and further illuminate the focus of the conversation. It should never confuse the teacher or muddy your overall message. In other words, think red or blue!

Think of indicators as artifacts or pieces of evidence. You want to give careful consideration when choosing indicators to support your C.R.A.F.T. conversation. Although you might have several indicators in mind, you do not want to inundate teachers with artifacts. When you use too many indicators, it is easy to shift the conversation from a growth experience to one filled with anxiety or even embarrassment. Having too many indicators makes it seem like you are trying to "get" the teacher and not "grow" the teacher.

Indicators should also be current. The *T* in C.R.A.F.T. stands for *timely*, and that reminds leaders to use artifacts that, when possible, are recent. Sure, you may have a teacher's summative assessment results from the last six years printed out, but you certainly shouldn't use that information to highlight a Depth of Knowledge concern this school year. When you provide teachers with up-to-date indicators, it shows that you are paying attention to their practice and that you are shedding light on something current that needs their attention. Having no indicators from the present or the immediate past should serve as a warning that your assertions are not well supported and you might be planning to take the conversation in a direction that it does not need to go.

It is also important to make sure indicators are easy to comprehend and pinpoint the focus area in a nonbiased manner. For example, let's say that you have a conversation coming up with Mr. Greene next Tuesday. You want to speak with him because you have received several complaints from parents about his questionable grading practices. Some leaders might think it is a good idea to print out some of the e-mails so Mr. Greene can understand the issue. However, although the e-mails pinpoint a trend, many of them could be biased, and it might be difficult for Mr. Greene to plainly see the issue.

Instead, as part of your planning process, you should gather quality indicators. An example in this case might be a copy of one of his graded quizzes that consisted of one question and allowed a student to earn a score of either 100 percent or zero. Perhaps you might print out a copy of his gradebook, which shows that tests are worth 40 percent of a student's grade but only one test was given over the entire quarter. These types of indicators help to enlighten and bring clarity.

It is also advantageous to select indicators that will have the biggest impact. Perhaps there is one indicator that could help illustrate two points that you are trying to drive home. For example, a parent e-mail might highlight a teacher's grammar challenges as well as his or her need to be mindful of tone in online communication.

The presence of indicators ensures that your conversation is not built merely on opinions, hearsay, or emotions. Nothing is worse than having a conversation with a teacher in which you are making claims without any supporting indicators. Again, if you have no quality indicators, rethink having the conversation. Here are some quality indicators to consider when planning for a C.R.A.F.T. conversation:

- E-mails
- Lesson plans
- Gradebook reports
- Observation notes
- Classroom video

- Anecdotal notes
- Student work
- Classroom pictures
- Data reports
- Sample tests and quizzes

Cornerstone Questions: *Promoting Collaboration*

Collaboration should be evident throughout the engagement component of every C.R.A.F.T. conversation. Just as listening and inquiry provide a space for leaders to become thought partners, so does the presentation of artifacts. It is not about slamming papers down on a desk; it is about having a tangible source of information that will promote further analysis and encourage collaboration with leaders and teachers alike. This set of cornerstone questions can be useful before, during, or after any C.R.A.F.T. conversation:

- Does the teacher see you as a collaborator? If not, what steps can you take to establish more of a partnership?
- How can you build on the teacher's existing ideas or thoughts?
- What tools can you use within the conversation to encourage collaboration?
- What collaborative opportunities has the teacher participated in previously that, if continued, could help that teacher reach the specific goal?

• In what ways can you encourage ongoing collaboration with the teacher?

Often, the C.R.A.F.T. conversation is the first time the teacher has the time and space needed to really collaborate with leadership. C.R.A.F.T. conversations create a one-on-one setting that makes collaboration natural and authentic. If leaders approach collaboration thoughtfully, they can help teachers see its value and make it something that they love to do.

Expertise

Although this notion might seem strange, expertise—accomplished skills or knowledge—should always come last in a C.R.A.F.T. conversation. Putting it last is easier said than done, however. After all, leaders have so much experience and valuable knowledge that they have acquired. It's instinctive to want to share that information and to simply "fix things" by telling teachers exactly what to do. Although directives are absolutely necessary in some cases, more often, teachers are able to come to their own solutions when listening, inquiry, and indicators are blended thoughtfully into the conversation.

Although expertise is situated at the bottom of the Core Four triangle, it is still an important piece for connecting the dots for teachers. Many teachers have a strong desire to hear your thoughts and to better understand what life was like for you when you were a classroom teacher. In many ways, the practice of sharing expertise helps to humanize leaders. Sharing your own personal anecdotes and experiences adds authenticity to the conversation and often helps calm the teacher and make him or her more open to critical feedback. However, you want to always remember that the teacher, whether novice or veteran, brings expertise to the table as well.

The act of sharing your expertise should be extremely intentional. It is easy to start sharing a story and to end up someplace you did not intend to go. Don't forget that the *A* in C.R.A.F.T. stands for *appropriate.* You want to make sure that what you choose to share is aligned to the focus and goal of the C.R.A.F.T. conversation. It also needs to be meaningful to the teacher at the current stage of his or her career. For example, if you're discussing classroom management with a veteran teacher who is new to your school, it would not be appropriate to share an anecdote from your first year in the classroom.

It is also beneficial to make the anecdote personal, when possible. Teachers respond well when leaders tell stories about themselves and not necessarily stories about past teachers whom they have coached or worked alongside. Ask yourself, "Have I experienced this in the classroom?" or "How have I successfully handled these situations in the past?" This is the time to be open and honest with your teachers, admitting to challenges you have faced or even things that you are still diligently working on. Don't shy away from real stories, and definitely don't share anything that is not true. Even as a leader, you have not encountered every situation possible. It is OK to say, "I did not personally experience this while teaching, but my grade-level chair did. Let me share with you how she handled it." This lets the teacher know that you are sharing "borrowed" expertise.

Sometimes the expertise you share does not come from experience but rather from something that you read or watched. When using outside sources, make sure that they are credible and that you have first-hand knowledge of what the article or video highlights. For example, let's say that Ms. Lee is working through how to help her students answer word problems completely. It's not enough to Google "how to solve a word problem" and print out the first two articles for her to read. What if those articles recommend a method that goes against your school district's policies or are poorly written? A teacher's time is valuable, so do not waste it on something that is not meaningful. Make sure you have read or watched what you choose to share. Doing so sets you up to be an ongoing thought partner with the teacher as you work together toward established goals.

Sharing expertise is a two-way street, and leaders often find themselves in the position of being learners during C.R.A.F.T. conversations. Remember that teachers are always the experts when it comes to their own individual experiences, especially inside the classroom. After all, teachers spend more time interacting with students on a daily basis than do the leaders in the building. It is important to encourage teachers to share their personal expertise. Make it clear that you honor their acumen. You can do this using direct statements or even questions. It is your job to draw out what teachers know if they are not able to do it for themselves.

> ## Cornerstone Questions: *Prioritizing Celebration*
>
> As you consider the next set of cornerstone questions, which focus on prioritizing celebration, think about the amount of expertise that exists in your school. Leaders are often seen as the experts in the building—an assumption that makes sense. However, every teacher brings a wealth of knowledge that supports success in ways that are big and small. What can be celebrated now, and what will you and the teacher look forward to celebrating in the near future? Use the following questions to guide your reflection on celebration:
>
> • What things are evident in the teacher's practice that can be celebrated during the conversation?
>
> • What actions have you seen this teacher take that show his or her potential to achieve the specific goal?
>
> • Can this teacher articulate any individual strengths that will be helpful in attaining the goal?
>
> • What are the aligned student actions that can be celebrated as the teacher works toward the goal?
>
> • In what ways can you celebrate this teacher as he or she works toward the goal?
>
> How can you connect this set of cornerstone questions to your current practice? It is helpful to look at each goal in increments and to help teachers feel seen and valued along the way by celebrating success. It is equally important that teachers be able to identify their own triumphs and not be ashamed to celebrate themselves as a way to stay motivated and enthused.

Let's revisit the vignette at the beginning of the chapter. Rashad has planned diligently for his C.R.A.F.T. conversation. He is scheduled to meet with Lisa in her classroom during her planning period. Rashad wants to make sure he taps into the Core Four—Listening, Inquiry, Indicators, and Expertise. He spent some time reflecting on his own listening skills and is ready to employ some new strategies to make sure his listening is active. Rashad also plans to review data as a quality indicator. Next, he wants to make sure he poses questions to Lisa that are not leading but are still thought-provoking enough to uncover the need to change some of her practices. Finally, he wants to share some of his expertise but also allow Lisa the opportunity to tap into her own toolbox and experience as an educator.

Rashad: Hi, Lisa. Is this still a good time to meet?

Lisa: Sure. I guess so.

Rashad: Well, I'm glad we could get some time on the calendar to chat.

Lisa: Me too.

Rashad: First, I wanted to see if you have had some time to review your student data from the state test last year.

Lisa: No. I really don't look at it too much because my students don't need to pass it to be promoted. We've talked about it as a group in collaborative meetings, but I really just listen. I don't see how it really affects me, since I really just need to focus on getting students to pass my class.

Rashad: Tell me more about what you mean when you say that you really just need to focus on getting your students to pass.

Lisa: I mean, my students need to make *A*s and *B*s in my class. They need to be at the top.

Rashad: I see. Well, let's take a look at some data I pulled. Take a look and just tell me what you notice.

Lisa: Well, when you lay it out next to everyone else's, I see that my students don't look like they are where they need to be. I guess I've always just seen my scores as a part of the whole, not really separate. My grades for my students are always at the top. I rarely have a student who makes below a C in my class.

Rashad: Let's look at this graph that plots classroom performance side by side with state test performance. What do you notice?

Lisa: I notice that many of the students with grades in the middle are performing right in the middle on the state test as well. Also, I see that some of the lower-performing class grades match performance on the state test.

Rashad: Here is your class data from last year and the year before. What do you notice?

Lisa: I notice right off that it doesn't seem to match the other school data at all.

Rashad: Tell me more about what you see.

Lisa: My kids do really well in my class. Why aren't they performing at the top like their class grades show they should? I guess I'm a bit shocked, and I want to know what I can do to change that. My kids do really well in my class, and I want them to do well on everything that has my name attached to it.

Rashad: You mentioned that your kids are at the top. Why do you think students do so well in your class?

Lisa: I think it's because I care so much about them. I want my students to feel success, and I really make sure the assignments I give grades for are reasonable for them to complete and to get a good grade on. I don't really give homework because I found that they don't bring it back, and just one zero in the gradebook can really hurt a grade and the self-esteem of the student.

Rashad: While visiting your classroom over the past few weeks, I can see that you really do care about your students. Tell me about the feedback you give students on their day-to-day work.

Lisa: I usually have students score one another's papers while I call out answers. This gives them immediate feedback to let them know how they are doing. Then their papers get passed back after I put the grades in my gradebook, and they put them in their notebooks so they can use them to study for the test.

Rashad: That's an efficient way to get grading done quickly. They do get their grades right away by doing this. What type of feedback does this provide your students with?

Lisa: Pretty straightforward: *A, B, C, D,* or *F.* I guess it would be helpful to give them a bit more—something more individualized so they know exactly where they need to focus.

Rashad: Yes! I remember my first year of teaching. I never knew how I was going to get all the grading done that needed to get in my gradebook while still giving quality feedback to my students. I'm going to be honest: I wasn't very good at it! It took me a few years of picking the brains of the other teachers in my building to really figure out how to manage all of that. I certainly didn't learn it from my administrator! I finally landed on a method that my grade-level chair used, and it was perfect.

Lisa: I have no clue what other teachers really do for this.

Rashad: So what I want you to do, Lisa, before we meet again next week, is to take some time to ask your teammates about how they give feedback to their students. I think you'll discover some good ideas, and you can begin to determine which method of effective feedback will work for you.

Lisa: That sounds good. I just want my students to be successful.

Rashad: We all want all our students to be ready for high school and to be successful in all they set out to accomplish. One additional thing that will help is to really dig deep into the standards data from the last common assessment using this analysis form. I think it will help you see which standards you need to spend some more time on with your students. Does that sound doable by next week at this time?

Lisa: I'll try my best, and I think I can get it done by then. I really haven't looked at my own data, just ours as a school.

Rashad: Next time we meet, we'll talk more about the strategies you plan to implement to give personalized feedback to each of your students. There will also be time for you to share what your common assessment data has revealed. We can then work together to help you gain better alignment between your student data and classroom grades. How does that sound?

Lisa: Good! I'm going to analyze my common assessment data to find weaknesses that I can work on with my students. I'm also going to talk to my teammates and grade-level friends to see how they give feedback. Then we can move forward.

Rashad: Sounds great! We're both on the same page. Let's plan on next week—same time, same place. In the meantime, please stop by to see me if you have any follow-up questions or if you need some guidance as you start to dig into the standards analysis sheet I gave you.

Lisa: I'll do that. I think I'll be OK, but it's good to know that I can stop by for help if I need it.

Rashad: My door is always open. Thanks for your time today, Lisa. I'm looking forward to working with you this year.

The vignette and sample C.R.A.F.T. conversation in this chapter highlight how the Core Four—Listening, Inquiry, Indicators, and Expertise—work together seamlessly to engage leaders and teachers in a shared experience that is not built on titles or traditional notions of top-down approaches to leadership. Rashad is able to actively listen and to ask thoughtful questions that lead away from assumptions toward understanding. Indicators are not presented in a punitive manner but introduced in the conversation as a way to further analyze what is happening inside Lisa's classroom and to help her uncover what changes might need to take place. Rashad even offers his expertise by sharing a personal moment from his own teaching career. The engagement component is the most critical piece of a C.R.A.F.T. conversation, and the Core Four provide leaders with a formula that works.

Closing Thoughts

Engaging in C.R.A.F.T. conversations should always incorporate the Core Four: Listening, Inquiry, Indicators, and Expertise. It's not enough to say, "I'm a good listener." Practice to ensure that you are ready to listen *actively*. Remember that inquiry is much more than just asking questions. It's knowing what type of question to ask, when to ask it, and how to probe further. Paint a clear picture for your teachers using indicators. Indicators are vital to help teachers uncover their challenges and to support their work inside and outside of C.R.A.F.T. conversations. Finally, although there is no replacement for expertise—whether it be yours, teachers', or borrowed expertise from another notable source—don't make the mistake of letting it overshadow the other three components of the Core Four.

As we began this chapter, we reminded you that engagement is really the heartbeat of a C.R.A.F.T. conversation. It's where change and growth can take place for your teachers. Through careful thought and planning using the Core Four, you can ensure that you and your teachers are fully engaged in each conversation and working collaboratively toward a common aim. By the end of the conversation, both parties will be well informed and ready to work. In Chapter 5, we will take a closer look at the closing of a C.R.A.F.T. conversation. It's not enough to simply say, "Thank you for your time." As we unpack how to bring closure to a C.R.A.F.T. conversation, you will find the wise saying to be true: in every end, there is also a beginning.

5 | Successfully Closing C.R.A.F.T. Conversations

Silence is one of the great arts of conversation.

—Marcus Tullius Cicero,
Roman orator and statesman

INSIDE THIS CHAPTER:

- Outline Supports
- Identify Measures of Success
- Strive for Mutual Satisfaction
- Construct a Summary

Tina is excited about the start of another school year, especially when she discovers that she has a brand-new group of teachers to evaluate. After reviewing their self-assessments and making a reference sheet for each of the 10 teachers she is assigned to evaluate, she realizes that 8 of them are interested in honing their assessment strategies this year. This commonality becomes a focus area as Tina begins to plan for conversations with each of them.

Her first conversation is scheduled with Francesca, a teacher with more than 11 years of experience in the classroom. Francesca has been very forthcoming in her self-assessment about wanting to push herself out of her comfort zone and use a variety of assessment strategies instead of the typical paper-and-pencil tests and quizzes. Tina understands that their conversation will be the catalyst for helping Francesca reach her goal, so as she plans, she gives the closing portion special attention. Her planning needs to ensure that closing elements are included so both she and Francesca will leave the C.R.A.F.T. conversation with outlined supports, clear markers of success, mutual satisfaction, and a concise summary.

Closing a conversation may not seem like a big deal at first, but have you ever finished a conversation and thought, "I have no idea what to do next!" or "What just happened?" The closing of a conversation is often an afterthought—or not a thought at all. We simply exchange a few words, shake hands, and move on with our day-to-day lives at the end of most conversations. However, a C.R.A.F.T. conversation is not complete without a purposeful closing.

It might help to think about the closing of a C.R.A.F.T. conversation the same way you want teachers to think about the closing of a lesson. You've probably observed hundreds of teachers who were mid-sentence when the bell rang and watched as students packed up and dashed out of the room. Needless to say, you probably weren't pleased. Well, can you remember a recent conversation in which you simply ran out of time? Or can you recall a conversation in which you know the teacher walked away more confused or disgruntled than when he or she entered the room? This happens all too often in schools because leaders do not prioritize the closing of the conversation. Excellent teachers put time and energy into planning how they will close a lesson using summary strategies and other best practices. Leaders must use a similar approach when closing a C.R.A.F.T. conversation.

Although the closing might last only 5 to 10 minutes, it is the piece of the conversation that ensures that the teacher and the leader will have the force and the focus needed to put their words into action. To successfully close a C.R.A.F.T. conversation, leaders must adhere to the Final Four: Outline Supports, Identify Measures of Success, Strive for Mutual Satisfaction, and Construct a Summary.

Figure 5.1 illustrates the four overlapping segments that create the closing of a C.R.A.F.T. conversation. Notice that each of the four elements starts with a verb, which indicates action. The closing is not supposed to be a lethargic checking off of boxes. It is a vital part of the conversation and should be used as a push toward the goal. Think about planning intentionally to end every conversation using the Final Four, and in no time you will be delivering strong, well-planned closings.

FIGURE 5.1

The Overlapping Nature of the Final Four

Although each component of the Final Four has its own value, they are meant to work together. As you move through the summary of your conversation, you might find that the components begin to overlap as you and your teacher seamlessly move back and forth from one element to another. That's a great sign. When all four have been completed, you can be sure you have hit a C.R.A.F.T. conversation home run!

Outline Supports

As the engagement portion of the conversation ends and the closing begins, leaders must shift their focus toward the future. Each

C.R.A.F.T. conversation begins with a unique purpose, and through listening, inquiry, indicators, and expertise, a clear goal or set of outcomes is established to move the teacher in the right direction. The primary objective is to determine the specific and specialized ways in which you and others can help the teacher to reach a unique goal or goals. Throughout the conversation, you or the teacher might mention some actions needed to reach the goal.

For example, maybe the teacher suggests doing a lesson study with her department chair to strengthen her lesson-planning skills. Perhaps you suggest that the teacher read a few chapters from the book *Teach Like a Champion* (Lemov, 2010) to fine-tune her classroom management in key areas. Up to this point, everything is a mere suggestion or idea. The closing of a C.R.A.F.T. conversation calls for you to outline supports in a succinct and definitive manner.

Every teacher needs support, particularly when trying to improve classroom practices. The first part of closing a C.R.A.F.T. conversation is to clearly define supports. There are three key items to remember when determining how to support your teachers. First, be sure that every support is aligned to the prescribed goal or outcomes. Second, select each support with the individual teacher in mind. Third, provide the support in a collaborative manner that includes you, the school leader, and other teacher leaders in the building.

Alignment is critical when outlining supports. As leaders, we have our own toolbox of teacher supports, and sometimes it's tempting to just reach down, pull something out that has worked beautifully with numerous other teachers, and run with it. For instance, many leaders make observations their go-to choice. However, observation is not always the best way to offer support. Let's say a teacher needs assistance with developing summative assessments. Is an observation really going to offer the teacher the guidance and help she needs? Thinking back to the *A* in C.R.A.F.T., remember to always keep the support *appropriate*. The only way to do this is to concentrate on the chosen goal.

To help the teacher with crafting summative assessments, perhaps you decide to have her compare and contrast two summative assessments—one that is an exemplar and one that is not—and then have a conversation about what she noticed. Or maybe the teacher will watch a short YouTube clip on Depth of Knowledge levels before cocreating the first half of her summative assessment with her instructional coach.

There are many ways to assist teachers in reaching a goal. Make sure you choose aids that are worthwhile and will have a real impact. Notice that the focus is on *impact*, not necessarily *speed*. Sometimes the fast route gets us to where we want to be, but it leaves out the opportunity to build the teacher's capacity in such a way that the same work will not have to be repeated. Shortcuts are not allowed.

It is also important to select sources of support that are individualized. This can be difficult to do as a leader when you've seen success in a comparable situation. For example, let's say that last year you worked with a teacher in your school who struggled to communicate clearly with parents using his classroom website. You supported him by creating a WebQuest designed to have him look more closely at exemplar teacher websites and to determine two focus areas to improve his own website. Your support worked like a charm. Now that another teacher is in the same situation, why not support her in the same way? Although sometimes the same type of support should be replicated, it is important to think of each teacher as an individual. One size does not fit all.

As a leader you must ask yourself, "What type of aid is best suited to help *this* teacher reach the intended goal?" This is when knowing your teachers really comes in handy. If the teacher is a visual learner, the WebQuest might be perfect. If the teacher is an auditory learner, maybe the best support would be a great podcast you found on the "Top 10 Ways to Clearly Communicate with Parents." Have you ever heard the saying about "trying to fit a square peg into a round hole"? It just won't work! That is exactly what happens when you create supports that are not unique to each teacher and that teacher's goal. Here are various ways to support teachers:

- Referencing an article, a blog, or a book
- Providing coverage to observe master teachers
- Coteaching
- Offering professional development aligned to goals

- Providing exemplars of desired outcomes
- Viewing instructional clips or videos
- Delegating time with an instructional coach
- Establishing a peer coaching relationship
- Engaging in role-play

Once you and the teacher have determined the support needed, it's time to consider who will offer the support. Remember that the *C* in C.R.A.F.T. reminds you to always be *clear*. We want teachers to know exactly what they will be doing and who will be assisting them each step of the way. This is where the distributed leadership model can really come to life. As a leader, it is your job to know the strengths of your staff and to know who you can count on. Don't just think in terms of grade-level lead teachers and instructional coaches. That's a pretty limited scope. The teacher across the hall might be the best person for the job, or sometimes it is advisable to shake things up by using teachers in different content areas or grade levels. If you're already thinking about how time could be an issue, consider collaborative uses of technology. Google Classroom and Google Docs are excellent avenues for teachers to share ideas, activities, calendars, and plans.

The one thing that is easily forgotten when selecting supports, particularly when using a distributed leadership approach, is *you!* As a leader, you are always going to have a laundry list of things to do. But as the number-one instructional leader in the building, supporting your teachers should always be a top priority and will always be one of the best uses of your time. Make the time. Get your hands dirty. Whether that means attending collaborative planning meetings, providing constructive feedback, or even coteaching a lesson, just do it!

Setting up supports is one thing, but garnering a 100 percent commitment from the teacher is another. It is advisable to let teachers know that it is ultimately their responsibility to take the help that is being provided. If your sources of support are aligned and individualized and encourage collaboration, you are already ahead of the game.

As you begin to work with your teacher toward a given set of outcomes, be sure to follow up and get feedback on how things are going. You might have to alter a source of support along the way or lengthen your time line—and that's OK. The important thing is to continue working until you reach the goal. Chapter 6 will guide you through the critical steps often overlooked when following up and delineate how to provide structured, frequent feedback.

Cornerstone Questions: *Promoting Collaboration*

As you determine how best to support your teachers, you will likely find that many of the most successful approaches will include other people. Whether it's coteaching or attending a professional development course, collaboration gives teachers the time and space needed to challenge old ways of thinking and the boost of confidence needed to do things differently. Use the following questions to guide your reflection on collaboration:

- What collaborative tools would be effective, given the specific goal?
- Which teachers in the building are considered experts in the given focus area?
- Does the support needed lend itself to a cross-curricular or vertical grade-level experience?
- What groups are already established in your building that offer accessible support on an ongoing, frequent basis?
- Are there external school stakeholders who could lend resources or aid aligned to the goal?

Collaboration is paramount as you work to aid and support teachers. Let these cornerstone questions guide you as you determine not only how to support your teachers but also who to involve. Sometimes the best sources of support already exist, such as a monthly PLC on differentiation. In other cases, it is helpful to survey your building and to really think about the individuals who are best suited to collaborate with teachers as they move closer to their goal.

Identify Measures of Success

No one wants to fail. Even as you open a C.R.A.F.T. conversation, you are doing so with the belief that success is inevitable. But often the teacher might not be entering the conversation with the same amount of positivity, hope, and determination. If you have planned and executed your C.R.A.F.T. conversation well, your teacher should feel uplifted and fully capable of making a change by the close of the conversation. In other words, the teacher should feel confident that success is well within reach. Reaching this point is half the battle.

Although being confident is crucial, it is even more valuable for your teacher to be able to identify concrete measures of success along the journey. Many leaders think that it is overwhelmingly obvious what success should look like, but this is not always the case. Often what the leader sees as success along the way does not align with the teacher's vision.

For example, Mr. Callahan has been giving his students daily homework that consists of worksheets with nearly 40 math problems. During your C.R.A.F.T. conversation, you discussed the purpose of homework and the concept of meaningful homework assignments. Two weeks after the conversation, you notice that Mr. Callahan has reduced the number of problems to 30 and assigns homework only three times a week. When you follow up with him, he is excited about his changes. Needless to say, you are not.

It is important that the teacher's and the leader's visions of success are completely in sync. To make that a reality, measures of success should be determined collaboratively at the close of a C.R.A.F.T. conversation. There are three important things to remember when identifying success markers. First, all success markers should be agreed upon. Second, measures of success should be embedded throughout the journey to improvement. Third, success can and should be measured in a variety of ways. Let's look at each of these more closely.

It is vital that you and your teacher agree completely about each measure of success. One of the best ways to ensure this is to start with the teacher voice first. Simply ask, "How will you know that you are being successful?" or "What does success look like for you and your students?" In most cases, teachers will have very solid answers to these types of questions. If not, you might have to probe further or offer an idea of your own.

As the leader, you should relish the role of thought partner at this time. Many teachers find this process a bit overwhelming or will naturally want you to tell them exactly what you will be looking for and when. This type of direct approach may be necessary in some urgent cases, but make sure that approach is dictated by the situation and not by the clock. Don't worry! Time will be on your side in the long run. When the success markers are agreed upon, you and the teacher can both feel good about moving forward and will be able to recognize with absolute clarity when things are going well or when things are going awry.

Have you ever suggested that a teacher give a summative assessment without giving any formative assessments along the way? No way! You can look at measures of success the same way. It is not advantageous for a teacher to have a measure of success that can only be realized once the goal is achieved. What will motivate this teacher along the way? What can the teacher point to and say, "I'm headed in the right direction. Things are happening!"? Success markers should be embedded along the way to the goal. This approach keeps the teacher motivated and the leader invested.

For example, Mrs. Kwan's goal is for 85 percent of her students to pass the county's quarterly benchmark exam at the end of the first semester. It is easy to think only about the end game: success equals 85 percent of her students passing. However, think about all the things that must happen on the way to that goal to make it achievable. When Mrs. Kwan can unpack a standard completely, that's success. When 90 percent of her students regularly ace the questions on the exit tickets she distributes as they leave her classroom, that's success. When 75 percent of her students nail the constructed-response questions, that's success.

As you work with your teachers at the close of your C.R.A.F.T. conversations to determine success markers, recall that the *R* in C.R.A.F.T. reminds us to be *realistic*. Think about what is possible for this teacher and at what point. When success markers are gradual, you can acknowledge small victories while working toward the larger goal.

As a leader, you must also keep in mind that success cannot be measured in just one way. In so many schools today, quantitative data is the only way to show success. We base everything on numbers. That's not to say that success should not be measured using numerical values or that quantitative data is not valuable to examine. Everything has a time and a place, and the *F* in C.R.A.F.T. reminds us to be *flexible*. Leaders need to push themselves to think about the variety of ways in which success can be shown, and some of those ways might be qualitative or a bit unorthodox.

Let's take Mr. Brown's last-period class, for example. You notice after several observations that instructional time is not being maximized. Students trickle in, and not much happens for the first 10 minutes. By the time the dismissal bell rings, Mr. Brown has barely gotten through half of his lesson plan. During your C.R.A.F.T. conversation, you both determine that the goal is to make the first five minutes and the last five minutes of his class effective and purposeful. Will success be best measured using numbers? Probably not. Student anecdotes might be solid measures of success, or even a video that shows that one minute into class every student is seated and working on the "Do Now" assignment.

By determining measures of success at the close of a C.R.A.F.T. conversation, you are providing teachers with a roadmap to the final destination. They can see clearly what success looks like along the way and can have incremental celebrations as they move closer and closer to the goal. You have also given yourself a great gift. No extra time is needed, and no guesswork has to take place as you follow up with teachers continuously. You too have clarity and focus.

Cornerstone Questions: *Invoking Change*

Change in school is often approached incrementally, with small steps taken over time eventually leading to large-scale change. This approach makes support over time vital and requires leaders to be able to identify small victories. The following cornerstone questions are designed to help you think about how supports and success markers are directly aligned to invoking change:

- Which of the outlined supports are job-embedded?
- How have you ensured that the success markers are incremental?
- How have you ensured that the success markers are aligned to the goal?
- Does the teacher have any school-related responsibilities that could be a distraction from the work required to make the change?
- What tools or resources will be needed such that the desired change becomes an integral part of the teacher's practice?

These questions focus on the individual teacher and that teacher's role in making unique changes that benefit students and the greater school community. It is important for leaders to provide teachers with the time, tools, and encouragement needed to make change possible.

Strive for Mutual Satisfaction

Any time a school leader and teacher sit down for a C.R.A.F.T. conversation, they both come to the table with expectations. Whether these expectations are high or low, hidden or disclosed, both parties have an idea of how they would like the conversation to proceed. When we discuss satisfaction, particularly mutual satisfaction, we are really asking, at the most basic level, "Did you get what you came for?" At the close of a C.R.A.F.T. conversation, it is important to make sure needs have been met and both parties are leaving the conversation with their tanks full.

Although it might seem like a great idea to just ask the teacher, "Did this conversation meet your expectations?" this type of loaded question can catch teachers off guard and be hard to answer when so many things have been discussed. Even if teachers tried to answer the question, many would say yes for fear of appearing disrespectful or potentially angering their boss. Ensuring mutual satisfaction is a bit more complex than asking a closed question. Leaders must bring the purpose of the conversation back to the forefront, participate in and encourage reflection, and try to answer any lingering questions. It's important to aim for the goal of meeting all parties' realistic expectations.

Mutual satisfaction cannot happen if you don't take the time to circle back to the initial purpose of the C.R.A.F.T. conversation. The purpose was determined before any discussion. It helped you plan for the conversation and has been the driving force behind the work you and the teacher have done. If the purpose has not been achieved, no one should be satisfied.

The best way to work through this process is to take a moment and restate the purpose of the conversation. For example, a leader might say, "I am so happy, Ms. Myers, that we had time today to discuss the need for more rigor in your AP Chemistry class." It is also a great idea to let the teacher lead by asking, "What was our motivation for meeting today?" When both the leader and the teacher are clear on the original aim for the conversation, determining whether the purpose has been achieved becomes effortless. The purpose then becomes a catalyst for reflection.

Appropriately reflecting during a C.R.A.F.T. conversation might require a period of silence. Silence in any conversation is often resisted and can make both parties uncomfortable or anxious. "Filling up" silence is a learned behavior, even if you do so with irrelevant discussion. C.R.A.F.T. conversations require leaders to honor silence and to use it as an opportunity for internal dialogue and reflection. Quiet reflection provides time for you and your teacher to think critically about the conversation and the work ahead. It can be tempting to skip this portion of the closing, but reflection is the linchpin of mutual satisfaction.

If you are worried about the silence feeling awkward, cue up this segment by saying something such as this: "After lots of discussion, it is good to simply take a moment to be quiet and reflect. Let's take the next two minutes to do just that." Remember that there is no rule book for reflection. Maybe your teacher will spend the time reviewing notes or jotting down lingering questions. Maybe you will take a moment to stare into space as you reflect on the first measure of success. It is a personal choice as to how to best use this time. Just make sure to use it.

After reflection, teachers often have lingering questions. They might be apprehensive about asking these questions because they are aware that the conversation is ending and time is short. However, when mutual satisfaction is your goal, you want to focus on the now and answer as many of those questions as you can. You will find that the best way to begin is by asking, "Do you have any final questions that I can answer before we go?" Or you can be more specific by saying, for example, "Now let's take a minute or two to go back through our checklist of supports and our time line to see if you still have any lingering questions." Teachers should understand that this is not the time to ask tough or convoluted questions. The questions asked during the closing of a C.R.A.F.T. conversation should be easily answered in a sentence or two.

If you find that your teacher is asking questions that require extended responses, it is OK to let him or her know that there is not enough time for you to respond appropriately and you will circle back soon. This is also an opportune time to provide any "quick fixes" that might be appropriate. Let's say that the teacher mentioned during the conversation that she is always getting e-mails from parents about their unawareness of scheduled tests and quizzes. You might reply, "You mentioned earlier that parents don't know about tests. Check into using the Remind app. I think it might help." You should not try to fix every problem the teacher mentions. In fact, you might not have any quick fixes at all. Regardless, keep in mind that quick fixes are small things that can be helpful to the teacher without requiring loads of time and energy.

Let's face it: not all your C.R.A.F.T. conversations are going to end with both or even one of the parties being satisfied. However, if you circle back to the purpose, make time for reflection, and answer any final questions that the teacher has, then mutual satisfaction can be achieved. Be sure to keep your tone positive and encouraging as you work through this segment of the closing.

?
!

Cornerstone Questions: *Prioritizing Celebration*

Mutual satisfaction at the end of a C.R.A.F.T. conversation does not mean that teachers leave overjoyed. It means they leave with an understanding of what needs to be done and why it is of value. If the *why* is clear, the *how* becomes easier. When teachers are equipped with this knowledge, goals become attainable and celebration becomes inevitable. Use these questions to guide your reflection on prioritizing celebration:

• What are ways that the teacher can be celebrated for achieving each measure of success?

• What are ways that the students can be celebrated for achieving each measure of success?

• When the overall goal or set of outcomes has been achieved, how will you celebrate the teacher?

• What are some ways to celebrate those teachers, leaders, and stakeholders who are working collaboratively with the teacher?

• Are there county or district celebrations that coincide well with the goal?

This set of cornerstone questions reminds leaders to celebrate small successes and to look at celebration in a holistic manner. Although the teacher has an individual goal, it is imperative for leaders to look for opportunities to celebrate the teachers' students and colleagues who are playing influential roles in their progress.

Construct a Summary

If you have had a quality C.R.A.F.T. conversation with your teacher, then a lot has occurred in a short time. You have taken part in discussion, critical thinking, probing, and so much more. Even if you both have been fully engaged and one of you has been taking copious notes, it is easy for key items to get lost or forgotten. When you are closing a C.R.A.F.T. conversation, you must take time to construct a summary. Summarizing the conversation entails providing a clear and concise review that gives the teacher the clarity and confidence needed to act.

Often the most challenging part of constructing a summary is simply getting started. At times, the conversation naturally leads into the summary, but often the leader will have to shift the conversation in that direction. It's perfectly fine to send a cue by saying, "We are almost out of time, and I want to make sure we leave our meeting with a mutual understanding" or something like "I love the direction we are going and I hate to lose our momentum, but there are a few quick items I want to review before our time is interrupted by the bell." These types of prompts let teachers know where the conversation is headed while simultaneously sending a message that their input, expertise, *and* time are of value. Once you have shifted the conversation and are ready to construct a summary, there are a few things to keep in mind.

Do you remember sitting at your desk when your 6th grade teacher taught a lesson on how to write a summary? We hope you were paying attention! One of the things that your teacher probably noted was that a summary is not a rewrite of the original piece. It's likely that he or she also highlighted that a summary includes key points and not minute details, and it should not be too long. Who knew that your language arts teacher was preparing you for C.R.A.F.T. conversations? These are the most critical things to keep in mind as you summarize the conversation.

You may remember the Cliffs Notes study guides, with their black-and-yellow-striped covers, or you may be familiar with one of the most popular apps used by students today, SparkNotes. SparkNotes is an online resource that mimics the Cliffs Notes of the past, enabling you to do a quick search for a summary of a book in the form of one or two easy-to-read pages for each chapter. As you construct the summary, think of it as the SparkNotes of your C.R.A.F.T. conversation. You are turning a 60-minute conversation into a 160-second soundbite. Remember, the teacher was a part of the conversation as well, and you would be wasting the teacher's time and yours if you were to give a play-by-play of every topic, statement, and question. To construct the summary successfully, you must pay close attention to key portions of the conversation.

During the summary, you must feel comfortable taking the lead and bringing the teacher's attention to the details of the conversation. This is not the time for probing or a lot of back-and-forth discussion. The goal is for the teacher to leave the conversation ready to act. First, start with expectations. Let the teacher know what is expected of him or her in the future. This involves more than restating the agreed-upon goals or outcomes. Be specific and clear so there is no gray area. Teachers should know what they will be held responsible for after the conversation ends. You also need to remind teachers of the activities that they will be engaged in throughout the process. In other words, remind them of what's coming their way.

Many teachers might feel overwhelmed by the work ahead, whereas others will be excited. That's why it is key for you, as the leader, to focus on the *T* in C.R.A.F.T., which stands for *timely*. It's your job to help the teacher prioritize immediately. You should give special attention during the summary to a review of the next steps. What is the very next thing the teacher will do? For example, during your summary you might say, "Don't forget that you are going to kick things off by observing Mr. Hill on Thursday" or "I'll be sending you the link to the ASCD article we'll be reading so we can both be ready to chat about it next week." By reminding teachers of what's coming soon, you are setting them up for early success, which is vital to continuous improvement.

Timing is everything in a C.R.A.F.T. conversation, especially when you are often constrained by the ringing bells and transitions orchestrated down to the second in a school setting. The same thing can be said of summarizing your conversations. This is not the time to ask additional questions or to provide another anecdote to highlight how important the work ahead will be. The labor has already been done during the course of the conversation. You might feel like there is more to discuss or just one last comment that needs to be made. Don't give in to that feeling. The summary is designed to be brief. Keep it that way.

Closing a conversation can be challenging, especially if the conversation has been difficult and even if it has been thought-provoking and stimulating. It's a part of conversations that typically doesn't get a lot of time and attention. However, if you focus on closing effectively, you will see the difference it can make regarding teacher follow-through. Although there will be some overlap, leaders need to give attention to each of the Final Four segments as individual pieces to the larger puzzle. To close a C.R.A.F.T. conversation, you must outline supports, identify measures of success, strive for mutual satisfaction, and construct a summary.

Cornerstone Questions: *Building Capacity*

When the Final Four are embedded in your closing, you are setting the stage to build capacity in a way that is personalized, intentional, and sustainable. Consider the following set of cornerstone questions as you think about the Final Four and how important it is to bring each C.R.A.F.T. conversation to an effective close:

• In what specific area(s) are you hoping to build the teacher's capacity?

• Are the outlined supports proven to build capacity in the desired areas?

• What best practices should the teacher continue while working toward the goal?

• What new best practices will be introduced through the outlined supports?

• Are there leaders in the school who could build their own capacity by working collaboratively with the teacher toward the goal?

You can use this set of cornerstone questions to help build capacity in tried and true ways. Thinking outside of the box is awesome, but best practices are *best* practices for a reason. Make sure you are using current research and prior knowledge in pertinent ways that benefit your teachers and leaders.

Let's revisit the vignette presented at the beginning of the chapter and see how Tina uses the Final Four to close her C.R.A.F.T. conversation. She has planned her timing to ensure she has enough time to lay out supports for Francesca, and she has tailored the supports to meet the needs that Francesca specifically requested in her self-assessment.

Tina: OK! We're really on a roll. We've gotten a lot of work done, and I want to make sure we both leave the conversation ready to go.

Francesca: Me too!

Tina: Let's start by outlining supports. We've both given a few suggestions while chatting, but let's pinpoint exactly what type of assistance you'll need.

Francesca: I liked the idea of doing the assessment circle at our next team meeting. With all the teachers bringing in at least three types of ways they assess their kids, I'll get a lot of concrete examples and ideas.

Tina: Sounds good! I also know that you love reading articles and blogs. There's an article that I read that would be very informative. It even lists assessment types and ideas along with their pros and cons from a teacher and a student perspective. I think it will give you some additional ideas and things to think about before you narrow it down.

Francesca: Perfect! Between the support from my team and your article, I'll be ready to choose the two new types of assessments I'm going to use this quarter. When I meet with the instructional coach, she can help me fine-tune my strategies.

Tina: All right. Well, how will you know when you're being successful?

Francesca: Honestly, success will start with me choosing my two strategies and being able to discuss why I chose them and how they will benefit my students. It will also be a huge success when I roll out the strategies and I'm able to see how my students perform. This will give me great info on my instruction and on the assessment strategies.

Tina: I agree. I think the end-of-quarter survey can also be used as a success marker because students have to answer questions directly related to the assessments you give. You know students are not shy about sharing their opinions. We can also use the benchmark to measure success. It's a traditional assessment, but it can let us know if the other assessment strategies you used gave you enough quality information to alter your instruction to meet students where they are and to ensure that they mastered the standards.

Francesca: I could see that. I'm good with that.

Tina: So our purpose for meeting today was to discuss your self-assessment and to specifically determine a plan to help you grow in the area of assessment strategies. We've discussed a number of supports and how we'll measure success. Now I'd like both of us to take a minute or two for quiet reflection.

Francesca: That sounds good.

Tina and Francesca take time to reflect in a way that is meaningful to them.

Tina: Now that you've had some time to reflect, are there any questions that are top of mind?

Francesca: Actually, I was thinking about using more technology in the classroom and blending that in with my assessments. Mrs. Archer is always raving about those ActiVotes. Where can I get those?

Tina: We have three classroom sets in the media center. All you have to do is sign up, but I heard they book fast! Check in with Mrs. Rollins, the media specialist, sometime this week.

Francesca: Will do!

Tina: We've done some great work today, and I'm looking forward to seeing you assess your students in new ways. We're taking a bite-size approach and just launching two new strategies this quarter. Your assessment circle is not until next week, so I'll go ahead and send that article your way tomorrow.

Francesca: Cool. I'm feeling good about the direction this year. I've never received exemplary ratings in this particular area, and now I feel like that's achievable.

Tina: I'm feeling good about our direction too. Remember, this is not the only area we'll be working on this year, but I really see you exceeding and showing leadership on a consistent basis with most of the other standards. I think this will be your year to truly shine as an outstanding instructional leader in all areas.

Francesca: I've never been asked by an administrator about what I need to become even better at, so this is very different for me. I really appreciate being asked what I want and just being able to share my thoughts on what success will look like.

Tina: Well, know that my door is always open, and please reach out to me at any time if there is anything I can help with. You have my cell number, so please call, text, e-mail, or drop by anytime.

The opening vignette and conversations presented in this chapter focus on closing your C.R.A.F.T. conversations successfully. Say goodbye to the days of simply thanking teachers for their time and moving on to your next task. Tina and Francesca demonstrate how the Final Four allow both parties to end the conversation in a way that honors the work they have done. A proper closing provides the clarity teachers need to confidently move toward their goal, knowing they will be supported continuously.

Closing Thoughts

When closing C.R.A.F.T. conversations, keep in mind that careful planning with the Final Four—Outline Supports, Identify Measures of Success, Strive for Mutual Satisfaction, and Construct a Summary—will end the conversation on a high note, with the teacher ready to take action. A strong closing will help achieve the mutual satisfaction C.R.A.F.T. conversations hinge upon and place any goal within reach.

Chapter 6 examines the final components of C.R.A.F.T. conversations: reflecting and following up. We will discuss the importance of making both of these components ongoing as you work toward goals with your teachers. Finally, we will offer strategies to help you with each component in addition to presenting solutions to some of the more common issues leaders face.

6

Completing the C.R.A.F.T. Conversation Cycle

To listen well is as powerful a means of communication and influence as to talk well.

—John Marshall, Chief Justice of the United States Supreme Court, 1801–1835

INSIDE THIS CHAPTER:

- Understanding Ongoing Reflection
- Strategies for and Challenges Related to Ongoing Reflection
- Understanding Ongoing Follow-Up
- Strategies for and Challenges Related to Ongoing Follow-Up

Jesse is entering his third year as an administrator at Pebblewood Middle School. He worked with several mentors over his first two years as part of a district leadership program. Most of the constructive feedback that he received from his mentors centered on his lack of follow-up. Jesse knows that if he wants to develop his teachers, he will have to change the way he interacts with them, especially after a C.R.A.F.T. conversation.

The school year starts off great! Jesse is spending time reflecting in his office and is doing a much better job following up with his teachers as they work toward specific goals. Change is happening, and it is tangible! However, in October he hits a wall while working with Mr. Patel on the issue of classroom rigor. After four weeks, everything is still falling flat. Jesse knows that he needs to come out of his silo and try reflecting collaboratively with his team to ensure ongoing follow-up that will help Mr. Patel and his students to move forward.

In Chapter 5 you learned about the Final Four, the components used to close a C.R.A.F.T. conversation, and what that closing can look and sound like. Now it's time to think about what happens when the conversation is over. It should come as no surprise that there is more work to be done. The final two steps in a C.R.A.F.T. conversation act as the glue that provides your teachers with a cohesive experience designed to propel them and your school forward to meet the needs of students.

Take a moment and think about all the conversations you had with different teachers last week. The conversations likely varied in topic, time, location, and even tone. Some stand out in your mind, and others may be difficult to recall in any detail. To ensure that your C.R.A.F.T. conversations count, you must ask yourself two questions: How will I reflect? How will I follow up?

Reflection and follow-up are the final two components of the C.R.A.F.T. conversation cycle. Without reflection and follow-up, the cycle is not complete, and in many ways, you risk undermining much of the work that you have already done. Reflection and follow-up may seem simple on the surface, but once you add the adjective *ongoing*, they become more than just boxes to be checked off your list.

Ongoing reflection and follow-up take time, consistency, and resolve. In this chapter, you will learn the C.R.A.F.T. conversation definitions of ongoing reflection and follow-up, along with go-to strategies for engaging in each. You will also discover solutions to a few common challenges leaders face when trying to work through these processes amid their other responsibilities.

Understanding Ongoing Reflection

After your C.R.A.F.T. conversation ends, it's time to shift gears. Although the teacher will likely leave the meeting ready to take some immediate action, a leader's first task is to take a moment to begin the process of ongoing reflection. To understand exactly what this activity entails, let's take a moment to unpack the words themselves.

The term *reflection* is a noun that refers to significant thought, consideration, and deliberation. The word *ongoing* is an adjective that signals a purposeful process of continual thought and deliberation. When a C.R.A.F.T. conversation closes and ongoing reflection begins, the leader embarks on a journey of careful contemplation that continues as the teacher advances toward the goal.

At this point, you might be wondering why we chose to use the term *ongoing* reflection. Most good school leaders take time to reflect immediately after a conversation. They might jot down a few notes, or maybe they reflect during their drive home and stash some things in their mental file folder. Typically, the next day they simply move on, whether by choice or necessity. But leaders who want to have an impact and to see their teachers and students grow exponentially understand that reflection must continue over time. Ongoing reflection is a vital component of a C.R.A.F.T. conversation.

Have you ever thrown a pebble into a lake and watched as ripple after ripple is formed? It's a magical thing to observe as each circle appears even larger than the last, seemingly going on forever. Ongoing reflection works in a similar manner. It creates a ripple effect that begins with you and extends further to reach your teachers, your students, and even your larger school community.

The power of ongoing reflection is harnessed by you, the school leader. The first step is to look inward and to examine yourself. It is natural that early periods of reflection might center on you and your role in the actual conversation. You might ponder questions such as "What are the things I did that helped the conversation to be successful?" or "Mr. Brown seemed to shut down midway through the conversation. Did I balance expertise and inquiry?"

The next wave of contemplation will likely focus on the teacher and the agreed-upon goal. You might have thoughts such as "Ms.

Arnold seemed excited but still a little anxious. Would she benefit from a revised peer-observation form that is more succinct?" or "We agreed on a five-week time line, but change is happening swiftly. What are the other things Mr. Bailey is doing that are fast-tracking his progress?"

As progress toward the goal occurs, the process of ongoing reflection should continue. You might find your thoughts shifting from your role and the teacher's role to the students who are directly affected by the work. You may wonder, "What is it about the new strategy that is working so well for our ESOL students?" or "The entire 5th grade team has started using rubrics after Ms. Hunter's achievement gains. Can we adapt this technique for lower grade levels?"

It's not long before the effects of ongoing reflection reach beyond the students most closely associated with the goal to your entire school community. Reflection can contribute to success and achievement—effects that spread quickly and easily, especially in a school where building capacity, invoking change, promoting collaboration, and prioritizing celebration are a way of life. Each period of reflection is like a tiny drop of water starting the ripple effect over and over again. Figure 6.1 illustrates the ongoing ripple effect of a leader's reflection and how it eventually reaches teachers, students, and the community at large.

FIGURE 6.1

The Ongoing Ripple Effect of Reflection

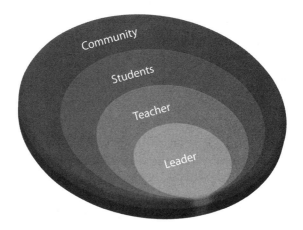

Cornerstone Questions: *Building Capacity*

When teachers take time to simply think about their students or their instructional practices, they are taking the first step toward honing their skills. As leaders follow up with teachers, they are providing them with the feedback and tools necessary for their growth. Use the following cornerstone questions to think about how reflection and follow-up help build capacity:

- How can you encourage teachers to make reflection a part of their day-to-day practice?
- How are you arranging your reflective notes to highlight trends and commonalities among your teachers?
- What strategies and techniques are you using to follow up with a specific teacher that the entire staff could benefit from (e.g., weekly e-mail reminders)?
- What technology platforms are you using for follow-up, and are there new and improved versions that should be introduced?
- How are you ensuring that your teachers are open to feedback?

These cornerstone questions can assist you in making reflection and follow-up an integral part of your school. You can use reflection as a tool to enhance teachers' practice and provide you with the time and space needed to individualize follow-up. As individualized follow-up takes place, you have the opportunity to adjust and use your insight to develop teachers on a consistent basis.

It is important to remember that the ongoing reflection process begins and ends with you. Now that you know what this process is and what it has the power to do, let's talk about exactly how you can get it done.

Strategies for Ongoing Reflection

As we've just described, ongoing reflection helps you to enhance your skills while simultaneously improving the work of your teachers, students, and the entire school. It is clear that ongoing reflection is worth the extra time and energy it requires. However, you might still be uncertain about exactly how to make it happen—a challenge that most leaders have faced. Among the many reflection strategies you can use, these three pair particularly well with the C.R.A.F.T. conversation experience:

• *Schedule time* to reflect, choosing a reflection method that works for you.

• *Document your reflections* to capture your most important thoughts and ideas.

• *Reflect collaboratively* to enhance innovation and ensure accountability.

Take a moment to think about these three strategies and your current practice. Is there a strategy that you already use? Is there one you've never tried or haven't quite been able to master? Although each technique stands alone as a best practice to help with ongoing reflection, the synergy among all three creates a reflection powerhouse. C.R.A.F.T. conversations are limitless when all three techniques are used effectively.

Schedule Time for Reflection

With time being one of our most valuable resources, we have to use it effectively and efficiently. Have you ever heard a colleague say something like "I've recently started to schedule my lunch. That's the only way I'll stop to eat"? At first, such a statement might sound silly, but when you think about it, the mere act of scheduling something makes it more likely to occur on a consistent basis. Ongoing reflection works in the same way.

Whether you use a digital service such as Microsoft Outlook or Google Calendar or a giant wall calendar, schedule time to reflect. Just as you would block out time for a meeting or a conference with a parent, pencil in time for reflection. Determine if your reflection time will be an hour after school or 15 minutes after the last lunch block. The time spent reflecting might differ from week to week, but the goal is to reflect continually.

It is also a good idea to determine exactly how you will reflect. The *R* in C.R.A.F.T. stands for *realistic*. It's important to be honest with yourself when it comes to reflection. What works for you? Reflection looks different for everyone. Some people have to have complete silence and close their eyes. Others may blast some music and dance around their office. Many leaders reflect better outside their school building and away from their spouse or kids, or talk to themselves on the drive home from work. How do you currently reflect? There is no right or wrong way to reflect as long as it works for you.

Document Your Reflections

When you take the time to reflect, an incredible number of ideas and thoughts may bubble to the surface. If we are being honest with ourselves, not all of those are worth remembering, but many are. Have you ever had a moment when you came up with a totally awesome idea? It might have been a hashtag for your next school fundraiser or a new way for Mr. Rhodes to approach a challenging student. You were so pumped, and the idea was so good, that there was no way you would forget it. How mad were you the next day when you could not remember it?

It is important to document your thoughts at some point during reflection. Whether it's midway through or at the very end, don't assume you will remember. Document it! You don't have to capture every word or idea, just the primary ones. Decades ago, you would have to have a pencil and paper handy to make this happen, but now you have various tools at your disposal. You can quickly type your thoughts into your cell phone notepad or use an app like Easy Voice Recorder to record them. If you love whiteboards, roll one into your office and cover it with ideas! You will thank yourself.

Reflect Collaboratively

Reflection in a silo works well for many people, and there is nothing wrong with engaging in the process alone. However, if you want to push innovation and build in a layer of accountability at the same time, try reflecting collaboratively. This technique is not recommended in the early periods of reflection, immediately after the conversation ends, but once the work begins, you might find collaborative reflection to be the best use of your time.

As teachers begin to make strides toward their goals, it is likely that other people in the building have partnered with them to provide help and support. Instructional coaches, team leads, and other school-level leaders will gain insight as they work with the teachers on a day-to-day basis. Having these individuals as thought partners can really take your reflection to the next level for a couple of reasons.

First, collaborative reflection tends to push your creative thoughts and open the door for innovation. Instead of posing questions to yourself, you are posing them to a team that is equally invested in the teacher's success. Everyone on the team brings different talents and experiences that influence the way they think and the way they approach certain situations. As thoughts and ideas are spoken aloud, the group's synergy brings forth new approaches and enhanced levels of critical thinking.

Second, reflecting with others holds you more accountable. When we reflect by ourselves, we often walk away with a list of things that we are going to do, but then we do nothing. We start to second-guess ourselves or tell ourselves that implementing the idea will take too much time or probably won't work. When our reflection time is collaborative, by contrast, other people have heard our thoughts and are excited for our ideas to come to fruition. Collaborative reflection makes it harder to not follow through. As leaders, we sometimes need that extra push.

Ongoing reflection is definitely easier said than done. Scheduling the time and selecting reflection methods that work for you is the first step. By documenting your reflections in a concise and accessible way, you are ensuring that your best thoughts and ideas will not be forgotten. When you are ready, take them to the team and use the power of collaborative thinking to transform your thoughts and make action a priority.

Challenges Related to Ongoing Reflection

Although the three strategies just described are tried and true, as you become a master of C.R.A.F.T. conversations, you might find yourself adding other techniques to your list. That's great! As you add more reflection strategies to your leadership toolbox, you will find that reflection becomes a prominent part of your leadership style. However, even leaders who achieve this will still face challenges. Here are a few of the most common challenges and some quick solutions:

Challenge #1: Unscheduled Interruptions

You have scheduled time on your calendar to reflect this week, but the time keeps getting interrupted. Whenever you take a seat and close your door, another fire appears that needs to be put out.

Solution: Tag in a team member! Who is your support? Whether it's an assistant principal or a counselor, let that person know that you will be scheduling reflection time and allow him or her to take the lead. As leaders, we often suffer from "me-itis." We think, "Everything must be solved by me"—which, most of the time, is not true. Bringing in one of your team members will allow you the time and space to reflect while also building the capacity of other leaders in your building.

Challenge #2: Plenty of Reflection Time with Nothing to Show for It

You are diligent in scheduling your reflection time and have chosen a reflection method that allows your ideas and thoughts to flow freely. By the end of your reflection period, you know that you reflected, but you don't really have anything to show for it.

Solution: Take a bite-size approach. Sometimes when we begin to reflect, our thoughts wander all over the place. It can be helpful to pinpoint one or two focal points for reflection time. For example, maybe you will reflect only on what you saw students doing during your last observation, or perhaps you will center your attention on what the teacher is still finding challenging when engaging in a new instructional practice. When your thoughts wander, bring them back in focus by reminding yourself what exactly you are reflecting on.

Challenge #3: Reflection That Leads to
Upsetting or Uncomfortable Realizations

You finally have a moment to slow down and reflect. As you begin to think and deliberate, you realize that you are in the wrong. It might be that you handled a situation during the conversation in the wrong way, or perhaps the approach that you championed does not align with the vision and mission of your school.

Solution: Be honest! Leaders often put extra pressure on themselves to be perfect. There is an unspoken expectation that leaders are all-knowing and will get it right every time. Recognize that you will make mistakes, and that is OK. Great leaders will acknowledge errors and will get beyond them by carefully explaining their initial thoughts. Great leaders model humility. By acknowledging a misstep, leaders can involve others in going back to the proverbial drawing board to rethink alternatives that lead to solutions. In other words, collaborative problem solving can emerge.

Despite the challenges, ongoing reflection is a powerful practice that can make a huge difference in your work with teachers. If you begin to think about working through a lens that includes reflective practice, you will naturally become accustomed to using C.R.A.F.T. conversations to push continuous improvement in your school. When paired with the last component of a C.R.A.F.T. conversation, ongoing follow-up, you will undoubtedly be leading your teachers and students toward an enhanced school culture.

Understanding Ongoing Follow-Up

Follow-up is critical for a C.R.A.F.T. conversation to run its full cycle and can make the difference when working with teachers toward meeting goals. Just as *ongoing* is an important descriptor of reflection in the cycle of C.R.A.F.T. conversations, it is also a critical aspect of follow-up. Ongoing follow-up ensures continuous time and attention is given to reaching the established goals. Ongoing follow-up is a purposeful process of layered communication designed to continuously support teachers in reaching established goals.

exac   *going,* but what
next   -mail to outline
level   :uss the grade-
leade   1 and complex
when   ation cycle.

Th   .....s to come after or to move
behind   ..... direction." The term *up* is an adjective defined as
"toward a more elevated position." When leaders engage in follow-up,
they are moving in tandem with their teachers toward a higher level of
effectiveness. Each subsequent follow-up activity builds on the last to
build momentum and to keep the teacher moving in the right direction.

The process of ongoing follow-up takes time and intention. Think
about how you currently follow up with your teachers and colleagues.
Do you casually say, "Let's talk again next week or tomorrow"? Do you
complete a classroom observation and leave a note with "grows and
glows"? C.R.A.F.T. conversations call for follow-up to be sustained such
that you and your team have multiple touchpoints with the teacher in
a variety of meaningful ways. As the last component of a C.R.A.F.T.
conversation, it allows leaders to develop a focus on one, if not all
four, of the foundational cornerstones: Building Capacity, Invoking
Change, Promoting Collaboration, and Prioritizing Celebration.

As an analogy, think about how much work is required for horti-
culturists to take crops from seed to table. They don't just sow seeds
outdoors or in a greenhouse and look to Mother Nature to handle the
rest. They don't abandon their greenhouses for long periods of time,
hoping that solar radiation will do their job for them. Horticultur-
ists understand that plants need continuous care and attention. They
work continuously to grow and harvest their plants year-round.

Leaders can think of ongoing follow-up in a similar manner. Just as
a horticulturist must continually follow up to ensure plants and crops
are progressing as expected, school leaders must frequently follow up
with teachers to ensure they are progressing toward the desired outcome. The power of ongoing follow-up centers around teachers being
seen and heard, leaders meeting teachers where they are, and leaders
having the ability to provide consistent, quality feedback.

Cornerstone Questions: *Invoking Change*

The following questions focus on the cornerstone of Invoking Change, especially as it relates to feedback. To make changes, teachers have to be informed and able to speak knowledgeably about what they are doing that is working and what might need to be tweaked. Feedback is central to change, and reflection and follow-up allow leaders to provide teachers with quality feedback and to ensure it is being used appropriately. Use these questions to reflect on feedback at your school:

- Do you believe that your school has a culture of feedback? Would your teachers agree?
- How do you ensure that your leadership team has a common understanding of what quality feedback is?
- What are your school norms for giving and receiving feedback?
- How are you holding teachers accountable after follow-up?
- What changes at the leadership level need to be made to better assist teachers in reaching their goals?

Think about how you can use this set of cornerstone questions to reflect on feedback within your school. Ideally, feedback should not be something that your teachers dread. It should be something that they look forward to. Once giving and receiving feedback becomes a common occurrence, follow-up becomes something teachers anticipate and desire.

Teachers want to be seen and heard throughout their professional journey, not just at the beginning and the end. You probably feel confident in your ability to have a C.R.A.F.T. conversation. You are also probably adept in determining whether a teacher has met the targeted goal. What about the dash in between? Follow-up allows leaders to check in with teachers along the way, using various approaches. By touching base with teachers as they progress toward their goals, leaders always have current knowledge of teachers' triumphs and challenges.

Current knowledge allows leaders to meet teachers where they are at all times. Even if your C.R.A.F.T. conversation was exceptional, the real work begins when the teacher starts working through the change. Things shift from day to day and week to week. Ongoing follow-up allows leaders to focus on what exactly a teacher needs and when. It might be necessary to change course and work in a more fruitful direction.

Remember that the *A* in C.R.A.F.T. is all about what is *appropriate* for each teacher. Appropriateness means not only that you should know your teachers and their goals but also that you need to stay rooted in current, research-based best practices.

When teachers are working toward a set of outcomes, it can be challenging to continue moving forward without feedback. Feedback is one of the most powerful tools you can use when trying to support instructional changes in the classroom. However, many leaders struggle to give quality feedback. Teachers want to know how they are doing and what they need to improve upon.

The *C* in C.R.A.F.T. reminds us of the importance of keeping things *clear*. Teachers appreciate feedback that is specific and helpful. Ongoing follow-up asks leaders to focus on not just what they are saying and how they are saying it but also on the tools they are using to do so.

As a leader, you might not know the science of plants, but you certainly know the science behind quality instruction. It is not enough to simply plant the seed. Leaders must use ongoing follow-up as a way to cultivate teachers' growth. Ongoing follow-up allows teachers to be seen and heard while simultaneously providing leaders with up-to-date knowledge that allows them to meet teachers where they are. Only then can leaders craft quality feedback that will lead to change.

Strategies for Ongoing Follow-Up

We all know how busy our days get. If you don't block off time in your schedule for follow-up activities, then they simply may not happen.

However, once you make ongoing follow-up a priority, it is vital that each touchpoint with your teachers be meaningful and impactful. A variety of strategies work well for follow-up, but these three rise above the rest when completing the cycle of C.R.A.F.T. conversations:

- *Use technology* to follow up independent of time and location.
- *Collaborate in groups* to bring teachers outside of their silos.
- *Offer varied, multimodal feedback.*

Before we examine these three strategies more closely, take a few moments to reflect on your personal practice when it comes to following up with teachers. Are the teachers you are currently working with actively moving in the right direction? How do you know that teachers are successfully implementing and using the supports you worked to put in place? If you found either question challenging to answer, it may be time to think about adjusting the way you follow up with teachers. As the last component in a C.R.A.F.T. conversation, ongoing follow-up provides teachers with the support and encouragement needed to keep their fire burning.

Use Technology

Whether you are entering educational leadership with just a few years of experience in the classroom or you have 20 years under your belt, the one thing that is guaranteed for everyone is change. It's important to keep up with changing trends not only in educational practices but also in the expanding world of technology. If you don't keep up with the trends, you may lose an opportunity to connect with your teachers.

When it comes to ongoing follow-up, technology can be useful to both you and your teachers. First, examine some of the technology tools that people in your school already use. For example, have any of your teachers used the Synth podcasting tool for professional learning? How many grade-level teams use Padlet to brainstorm collectively about ideas for project-based learning? Take a minute to think about how these same tools could be used to follow up with your teachers after a C.R.A.F.T. conversation.

Using technology to follow up allows you to touch base with your teachers independent of time and space, eliminating the need to schedule time to sit in a room to brainstorm. For example, Padlet would be an excellent tool to use to cocreate a lesson with one of your teachers. Whenever either of you has a thought or an idea, whether it's at 2:00 p.m. or 2:00 a.m., you can just open Padlet and jot it down! If you have a group of teachers working on a similar goal, you could use Synth to easily record a podcast that provides some instructional tips based on trends. Teachers can listen to the podcast on their way home or even in the shower.

Remember, today's new wave of teachers not only wants to use technology but also expects to do so. Available tools allow you to create everything from ongoing interactive discussion boards to time lines. The key is figuring out which modes of technology work best for the type of follow-up you are engaging in. Here are a few applications to preview and consider:

- Synth—an app for creating interactive podcasts to support digital learning and enhance classroom discussions
- Diigo—a Chrome extension that is a social bookmarking website allowing users to bookmark and tag web pages; users can capture and annotate online content to share with others
- MyHistro—an app that can be used for creating a time line, including steps and activities, documenting progress toward goals
- Timetoast—an app that can be used to create a storyboard to document past, present, and future goals for the year

Leaders can also use technology to help hold themselves accountable in making sure that follow-up is happening continuously. Remember the *T* in C.R.A.F.T. reminds us to always be *timely*. Timeliness is especially important in the "after the conversation" phase. Follow-up cannot be lagging. It must come at the appropriate time to keep the momentum strong.

Perhaps your school supports Google, and you are a fan of using calendar alerts to remind yourself of important things to get done. Maybe your leadership team uses the app Asana to keep track of who is supporting teachers, as well as when and how. We already know that if something is not planned, it's not likely to happen. Don't be afraid to use technology to help you schedule your follow-up work and stay on track.

Numerous tools are available to support your school with ongoing follow-up. It's hard to know where to start because so much is available for task management these days. Here are a few tools that you may want to preview to support timely follow-up:

• Toodledo—an online productivity tool to help manage to-do lists, take notes, track habits, and organize ideas into outlines and lists

• Asana—a web and mobile application to help teams organize, track, and manage their work

• Trello—a web- and app-based project management tool

• Remind—a communication platform to message individuals or groups to track appointments and ongoing follow-up

You may have decided that the variety of available tech tools is too overwhelming, but don't give up! Remember, technology is an innovation *and* an expectation. It can help you organize your time and connect with your teachers. Give yourself space to explore and discover which tools work best for you and your teachers. Technology is meant to help, not hinder. When used effectively, technology tools will increase your productivity so that you can follow up with teachers consistently and in a way that is not bound by time and space.

Collaborate in Groups

Much of what people do in schools is organized into teams. We have grade-level teams, content teams, and leadership teams. Why is it that we don't look at ongoing follow-up in a similar way? Have you ever conducted a series of classroom walkthroughs and then failed to find the time to follow up with those teachers individually? In many cases, individual follow-up is not the most advantageous way to reach teachers.

Let's say you observed a team of four teachers yesterday. When you reflected on your notes today, you were in awe when recapping how Ms. Carter summarized her minilesson. You quickly realize that at least two other teachers could really benefit from using some of Ms. Carter's strategies. Imagine the impact a group follow-up session, with teachers sharing and collaborating, could have on classroom instruction.

One of the best things you can do to effectively follow up in groups with your teachers is to strategically plan your path when visiting classrooms. For example, Rebecca evaluates the math department. After the last round of benchmarks shows some disappointing trends in geometry, she has a C.R.A.F.T. conversation with each team member to unearth what is happening and decides that each week she will visit the entire team on the same day. On Tuesday, all the geometry teachers are teaching translations and rotations, so she schedules classroom visits for all eight of them. The teachers have a common planning period, so the group follow-up session now becomes job-embedded. Instead of the planning time being wasted as teachers listen to what the leader has to say, it now becomes an interactive session as teachers discuss the lesson and what worked for their students. The leader's job is to probe only when necessary and to join with teachers in discussing possible next steps.

Collaborative follow-up is not always so neat. Recall that the *F* in C.R.A.F.T. calls for leaders to be *flexible*. C.R.A.F.T. conversations often reveal groups of teachers that vary both horizontally (across subject areas) and vertically (across grade levels). In these cases, the work ahead will mold your groups for you. These groups might even change as progress toward different goals is made. You will find that these mixed-group sessions are often richer and more thought-provoking than more homogeneous groups. However, you will need to get creative in scheduling the collaborative group follow-up.

What about hosting a breakfast meeting? Possibly your schedule allows for a lunchtime "Chat and Chew." You could host an after-school popcorn party. Teachers really appreciate small gestures, and the benefits typically far outweigh the cost. Don't forget about technology as well. Some of the tools described earlier can help with collaboration when time is scarce.

Cornerstone Questions: *Promoting Collaboration*

When teachers and leaders work together and value supporting one another in individual pursuits, collaboration is seen inside and outside of C.R.A.F.T. conversations. Collaboration during reflection and follow-up sustains the momentum and garners more unique and effective ways to help teachers reach their goals. The following cornerstone questions prompt you to look at reflection and follow-up in a collegial manner:

- What challenges are you facing as a school leader that could be addressed using collaborative reflection?
- What are some group norms that would be appropriate for collaborative reflection?
- What are some potential challenges you could face when following up with teachers in a group setting?
- How can you use technology to enhance meaningful collaboration among teachers working on similar goals?
- How are you helping teachers learn to give quality feedback to their colleagues?

These cornerstone questions can help you to define what collaboration should look like at your school as it relates to reflection and follow-up. The idea of reflecting in a group or following up in a group setting with teachers working on similar goals might be foreign to you. Start small by solidifying group norms and working with a team of teachers who are open to feedback and the idea of sharing challenges and successes with others.

Offer Varied, Multimodal Feedback

Feedback is an integral part of ongoing follow-up. You have probably read several articles or books on how to give feedback in terms of tone, verbiage, and clarity. All of these factors are important when providing your teachers with feedback. However, C.R.A.F.T. conversations require leaders to also think about feedback in terms of modality.

You can use a variety of methods to give feedback. One that is frequently overlooked is immediate feedback. Often, leaders look at feedback as something that happens later, but sometimes it needs to happen *now*. For example, if you observe a teacher delivering incorrect content or sharing the wrong definition of formative and summative assessments in a PLC, immediate feedback may be necessary. On the other hand, delayed feedback may be more appropriate if you have asked the teacher to respond to a written prompt after analyzing recent data. What about written feedback versus verbal feedback? Most leaders already use written feedback as part of their practice. However, you still have to determine if you will use pen and paper to draft a quick note or if you will send an e-mail with bullet points. Sometimes feedback is best given in a one-on-one setting, where you and the teacher can really dive deep. This method is particularly advisable when the feedback may be challenging to receive.

The idea is to figure out what needs to be said and then determine the best approach or technique to deliver the feedback. Here are a few useful feedback methods to consider:

- Face-to-face meeting
- E-mail
- Padlet
- Handwritten note
- Google Team Drives
- Comment feature in Word
- Blogs
- Discussion boards
- Interactive time lines
- Podcasts

Whatever method you choose for feedback, make sure you are prioritizing the most important information. Providing feedback is not an excuse to write an essay on what needs to be improved upon and how. You don't want to overwhelm your teachers. Think about time as well by considering digital resources that can provide a thoughtful exchange of ideas between you and your teachers.

Challenges Related to Ongoing Follow-Up

Simply put, school leaders must make time for ongoing follow-up. By using technology, collaborating in groups, and offering feedback in a variety of ways, leaders can hit the ground running. However, challenges will occur along the way. Here are a few of the most common challenges leaders face and ideas for how to combat them:

Challenge #1—Managing Meaningful Feedback Online

Teachers are required to blog weekly as a part of the follow-up to peer observations. This activity is an important part of meeting your school-wide goals, but you are struggling to give meaningful feedback on a consistent basis to all of your teachers. You are also concerned about providing feedback in an open online format.

Solution: Gather your team and set some norms! Identify some leaders in your building who can help. Do you have instructional coaches or grade-level chairs who could assist? This challenge could be a great opportunity to build capacity within your team. By asking other teacher leaders in your building to help, you are ensuring that quality feedback will be given on a consistent basis. Also, set some guidelines for the team about providing feedback using technology. You want to make sure that the tone and messaging are appropriate and aligned with your goals.

Challenge #2—Capitalizing on Great Instruction

You are faithful to your 5 x 5 schedule and conduct at least five walk-throughs each day of the week. You see so much great instruction, but there is never an easy way to share that with other teachers so that more students benefit academically.

Solution: Team up and use technology! Peer observations are not always possible. Use team and group settings that already exist to allow teachers to share strategies and ideas. Use your phone to record a clip of the instructional strategy you want to highlight and make a two-minute video. You can blast this out to your entire school for everyone to watch when they get a chance. If you feel that peer observations will work best for some teachers, consider how you are using your funds for professional learning. Dedicating some funding to substitute-teacher coverage for peer observations and follow-up sessions may be a better use of some of those funds.

Challenge #3—Making Book Studies Work

You really enjoy using book study groups to build capacity in your building. This year you have chosen a book that can be used as a tool for ongoing follow-up as well. In the past, book study groups have not gone very well, and you want to make this year's study successful, with robust dialogue and meaningful feedback. How can you go beyond chapter-by-chapter, round-robin sharing?

Solution: Pump up your protocols! There are numerous protocols for running effective book studies and similar efforts. Start with a quick web search and review several protocols to determine which one is best suited for your leadership style and your staff. Be sure to introduce the new protocol to staff members and let them get acquainted with it before the meeting. Using a protocol might be rough at first, but you probably will soon find that your staff enjoys it.

> ## ? Cornerstone Questions: *Prioritizing Celebration*
>
> The great thing about reflection and follow-up is that they both tend to shed light on people or things that should be celebrated. The following set of questions centers on the cornerstone of Prioritizing Celebration and will help you reflect on the way celebration already occurs in your building and how to use collaboration and technology to enhance its effects:
>
> • What are ways in which you can use ongoing follow-up to prioritize celebration?
> • What are ways in which you can use ongoing reflection to prioritize celebration?
> • How have you seen celebration play out in collaborative settings?
> • How can you use technology tools to help celebrate teachers' small successes?
> • What are some ways you've seen teams celebrate at your school that could become schoolwide practices for teachers and students?
>
> Use these cornerstone questions to guide your thinking as you begin to make celebration an embedded part of teachers' school experience. Keep in mind that celebration does not always begin and end with the leader. It is important to encourage teachers to use various resources to celebrate one another.

Despite the challenges, ongoing follow-up is the key to ensuring that teachers reach their goals with the appropriate amount of support. It keeps leaders engaged and up to date on what is really happening in the classroom and allows them to be the instructional leaders that teachers want and need. We hope that you already have some go-to follow-up strategies under your belt. There's no need to throw these away if they are effective. However, be sure to expand your horizons and make ongoing follow-up one of your top priorities.

Let's revisit the vignette presented at the beginning of the chapter. Jesse is all set to reflect with Carl and Katy. Carl is Mr. Patel's instructional coach, and Katy is a peer he wants to observe as he works to enhance his practices. Although Jesse is still a little hesitant about reflecting collaboratively, he knows he needs multiple voices at the table to push past the current roadblock.

Jesse: OK, everyone. Thanks for meeting with me today. I've really hit a wall with Mr. Patel, and I know that both of you have been working with him as well.

Carl: Definitely! I've been coaching him through some of the strategies before he tries them in his classroom.

Katy: I'm happy to help! He's done two peer observations so far, and we've had some informal chats about his takeaways.

Jesse: Well, I appreciate everything that the two of you have done so far to help. I'm not sure what we might be missing, so I thought it would be a good idea for us to reflect collaboratively to get some new ideas out there.

Carl: No problem. I see you have the whiteboard ready for us.

Jesse: Of course! I wrote *rigor* on it because that's our focus, and I want us to really stay on target.

Katy: I'll record what matters most as we reflect.

Jesse: Perfect! I want to start by making sure we're all on the same page with what *rigor* really means and what it looks like in the middle-grades classroom.

The group takes time to define rigor *and discuss look-fors.*

Jesse: We're on the same page, so let's jump in! What is going on, guys? What are we overlooking?

Carl: As Mr. Patel's instructional coach, I feel like we need to take a chunking approach. He's overwhelmed, even though he understands what *rigor* means. He's trying to make every single second rigorous and is getting lost. Let's chunk it.

Jesse: What part should we focus on?

Carl: I'd like to see him focus on the work period of the class—really honing in on what he has students doing.

Katy: That's a good idea. I feel like he has mainly observed the beginning of my class or the end, so he hasn't really seen the meat of the lesson.

Jesse: Really, Katy? I didn't know that. Good thinking, Carl. That's definitely a place where we could focus on rigor that will be impactful. I need to find coverage so that he can either observe a full lesson or at least the work period a few times.

Katy: Let me jot down "work period" on the board. I actually have a cool unit I'm launching next week, and the work periods are pretty varied. Because both of us teach science, I think it will help Mr. Patel to see different approaches that work for our content and kids.

Carl: Katy, I know you said you've had some informal chats after the observations. What do you think about setting aside some time to talk so Mr. Patel can ask questions and really unpack the different strategies you're using?

Katy: Sounds good! I know he mentioned wanting to do that, but it's hard to find the time.

Jesse: We can take care of that.

Katy: He also mentioned several times that he finds the peer-observation sheet distracting. It's just too long and doesn't work for him.

Carl: Maybe we can skip that part and just let him do his own thing?

Jesse: I'm fine with trying that, especially if we craft the follow-up conversations with you guys to be really focused and productive.

Katy: So, as two points of follow-up, we have peer observations with no form and scheduled chats after each one.

Carl: I think the point when I can follow up with Mr. Patel is after the observation. I just went to a workshop that focused on work-period instructional strategies. They gave us a packet of at least 20 strategies, many of which provide a high level of rigor. I planned to give it out to the whole team during our next PLC, and I think I can really leverage that with Mr. Patel.

Jesse: I'm scheduled to sit in on that PLC, so let's do that! I would love for us to discuss some of the strategies, and maybe we can even have all the teachers jot down one they want to try over the next two weeks.

Katy: That's perfect, because we'll all be trying something new. I think that will be very motivating to Mr. Patel.

Jesse: Me too! We're uncovering a lot of hiccups that have made it challenging for Mr. Patel to reach his goals. I want to add one more touchpoint. Because I'm a former science teacher, do you think it would be good for me to coplan a lesson with Mr. Patel? He will have observed the work period a few times, discussed different rigorous strategies, and selected a few techniques that he is excited about.

Carl: Yes! That sounds like a great way to collaborate with him, and I know he would be a bit nervous but super psyched that you're ready to roll up your sleeves.

Jesse: Perfect! Well, I think we have a solid plan. I appreciate you all taking time to reflect with me. Let's circle back in two weeks.

Consider the vignette and closing conversation in this chapter an example of how collaborative reflection can be used in schools. Jesse, Carl, and Katy are able to bring varying experiences and perspectives to the table to provide a more holistic view of the type of support that would be best for Mr. Patel. Leaders do not know it all, and it is important to see the value in reflecting with others to ensure that follow-up is ongoing and useful.

Closing Thoughts

The task of helping teachers achieve their goals really is a marathon and not a sprint. You can think about ongoing reflection and ongoing follow-up as those pit stops along the course where runners grab an energy drink to recharge and keep going. Even so, as the only two components of a C.R.A.F.T. conversation that happen *after* the conversation, it is easy to let them fall by the wayside. Resist the temptation! Stay the course! These two components really go hand in hand when working with teachers. You will find that your reflections will fuel your follow-up. The critical piece of the puzzle is ensuring that both activities are ongoing mile after mile.

Now that you have a handle on C.R.A.F.T. conversations, we will use Chapter 7 to highlight some of the most important takeaways. We will also discuss the importance of creating a school culture that is a fertile ground for C.R.A.F.T. conversations and the next steps for leaders who are ready to make C.R.A.F.T. conversations a part of their daily practice.

7 Are You Ready?

Leadership is an interactive conversation that pulls people toward being comfortable with the language of personal responsibility and commitment.

—John G. Agno, *What Is Leadership?* (2010)

INSIDE THIS CHAPTER:

- School Climate and Culture to Sustain C.R.A.F.T. Conversations
- Partnerships Paired with C.R.A.F.T. Conversations
- Rooting C.R.A.F.T. Conversations in the Four Cornerstones
- Setting C.R.A.F.T. Conversations Apart

When you step back and take it all in, you realize that C.R.A.F.T. conversations are not a big mystery. C.R.A.F.T. conversations provide a clear strategy for you as a leader to bring about open and honest communication in your school to support teacher growth and student achievement through building capacity, invoking change, promoting collaboration, and prioritizing celebration. When you focus on engaging in conversations that are clear, *r*ealistic, *a*ppropriate, *f*lexible, and *t*imely, you are able to work hand in hand with your teachers to help them reach their own unique goals. As individual teachers begin to achieve their goals, your school goals become more attainable.

As you start your personal journey with C.R.A.F.T. conversations, we would like to leave you with some final considerations and global takeaways to support you in your endeavor. First, we will take a moment to consider how your school's culture supports C.R.A.F.T. conversations and the value in leveraging other leaders and stakeholders to assist you as C.R.A.F.T. conversations become a way of life at your school. Next, we will dive into the four cornerstones for a final review to ensure you understand their individual and collective power. We will close this chapter by reviewing some of the key elements that make C.R.A.F.T. conversations unique and useful.

School Climate and Culture to Sustain C.R.A.F.T. Conversations

Often we hear the terms *school climate* and *school culture* used interchangeably. Although the terms share some similarities, it is important for leaders to be able to differentiate between the two when working with C.R.A.F.T. conversations. ASCD (2018) offers the following as a distinction:

> *School climate* refers to the school's effects on students, including teaching practices; diversity; and the relationships among administrators, teachers, parents, and students.
>
> *School culture* refers to the way teachers and other staff members work together and the set of beliefs, values, and assumptions they share. A positive school climate and school culture promote students' ability to learn. (para. 1–2, italics in the original)

Although nuanced in meaning, school climate and school culture are equally important when you are trying to build capacity through conversations. They are both key to unlocking the potential and power of C.R.A.F.T. conversations, and their influence has been addressed in Chapters 2, 3, and 6.

Emphasizing Relationships and Shared Norms

When you look at the definition of school climate just presented and think about it in relation to C.R.A.F.T. conversations, one of the first words that should jump off the page is *relationships*. In Chapter 3, we discussed relationship rules and outlined some things you must do to foster quality relationships with your teachers, such as claiming your baggage and giving your relationships the time and commitment they need to be sustained. The rules are also applicable to the relationships you have with the other leaders in your building. As you reflect on your school climate and culture and prepare to make C.R.A.F.T. conversations a way of life, focus on constructing and nurturing strong relationships in your building.

Culture is the bedrock of a school and is established through "shared beliefs, customs, and behaviors" (Clifford, Menon, Gangi, Condon, & Hornung, 2012, p. 3) that are "deeply ingrained" through "values and traditions" (Yesbeck, 2015, p. 1). Leaders play a pivotal part in building a positive school culture, namely by supporting and nurturing collaborative efforts with teachers (Drago-Severson, 2012). Bustamante, Nelson, and Onwuegbuzie (2009) share that school culture is "a learned system" including "norms, symbols, customs, behaviors, and artifacts that members of a group use to make sense of their world and foster a sense of identity and community" (p. 796).

The markers of a school culture—primarily norms, customs, and behaviors—tie into the work needed to build C.R.A.F.T. conversations that matter. Norms are essentially unwritten rules of behavior that in many ways shape how teachers communicate with one another. In their work, Saphier and King (1985) elaborated on 12 key norms that if present would, according to Zepeda (2017), grow a vibrant school culture. These norms range from fostering collegiality to holding absolute the importance of communication.

Norms are embedded in a culture. What can school leaders do to support the development of a school culture that fosters norms of collegiality and open lines of communication, with conversations at the center of teacher growth?

In its work examining leader and teacher development, Kadem Education, LLC (2019) has culled from research and practice a set of key drivers that, if attended to with fidelity, can support a school culture that is more responsive to teachers and their needs to grow as professionals—from the newest members of the school to more seasoned and veteran teachers. Figure 7.1 shows key cultural drivers that could support C.R.A.F.T. conversations by engaging teachers in substantive discussions with school leaders and with other teachers.

FIGURE 7.1

Cultural Drivers and Descriptions

Cultural Driver	Description
Clear & Unified Direction	The school's vision, mission, and beliefs (school's direction) are important in developing universally understood norms, practices, and policies. Programs are monitored for effectiveness in supporting the school's direction.
Professional Engagement	Teachers are lifelong learners necessitating multiple opportunities for them to engage in professional activities both collectively and individually. Conversations are created throughout the system to improve practice while modeling the attributes of a learner.
Instructional Autonomy	Teachers have the flexibility to make decisions about the success of each student using multiple metrics. Standards determine the core framework for teachers; however, flexibility, innovation, and personalization in instructional design are encouraged, supported, and shared.
Collaboration	Collaborative planning is required to develop and share instructional resources, and to embed the professional learning needed for expanding and improving teacher practices. New instructional designs emanate from shared expertise and support in using new instructional designs, and then evaluating their effectiveness.
Empowerment	Teachers have the responsibility to make individual and collective decisions that impact the school and classroom. Teacher voice and expertise are valued as an integral part of solving problems, developing school improvement processes, and planning their own professional growth.
Feedback & Reflection	Pervasive instructional observations provide immediate feedback and create conversations about effectiveness. The use of examples from practice and reflection activities provide clarity for professional growth.

(continued)

FIGURE 7.1

Cultural Drivers and Descriptions *(continued)*

Cultural Driver	Description
Resource Priorities	Teacher strengths and student needs are aligned in developing schedules that maximize teachers' skills. Shared selection of resources is leveraged to activate innovation and support teachers in meeting the varied needs of students.
Support & Care	Experienced teachers are valuable in providing support and mentoring to their colleagues. Meeting teachers' personal and professional needs through focused professional learning with follow-up are essential for professional growth.
Sense of Belonging	The feeling of being valued and part of the school brings meaning and importance to teachers' work. Teachers avoid working in isolation when they feel a sense of belonging. Diversity is valued, and programs are in place to make teachers feel like they belong.
Advancement	Opportunities are created for teachers to be leaders and experts in their fields. Career advancement is fostered through professional learning and innovations that lead to new professional opportunities.

Source: From "Cultural Drivers and Descriptions," by Kadem Education, LLC. Copyright 2019 by Kadem Education, LLC. Reprinted with permission.

Embedded in these drivers are actions school leaders can take to influence the development of a healthy school culture that advances trust and open-ended interactions. Recall that C.R.A.F.T. conversations aim to support teachers and leaders as they explore perspectives and ideas, uncover misconceptions, and collaboratively problem-solve in a *c*lear, *r*ealistic, *a*ppropriate, *f*lexible, and *t*imely fashion. To shape a healthy culture, conversations are needed to build capacity, invoke change, promote collaboration, and prioritize celebration.

Establishing a culture in which C.R.A.F.T. conversations are at the forefront is the goal. The way you choose to embed C.R.A.F.T. conversations consistently into your day-to-day practice is up to you. However, school culture hinges on what the staff believes and values, including norms, and more specifically, the norms that shape and guide patterns of communication—C.R.A.F.T. conversations. If you want C.R.A.F.T. conversations to become a part of your school's fabric, teachers must see the value of such conversations in their lives and the lives of their colleagues and students. Building value, like building trust, will take time and commitment.

If you had to sum up the current climate and culture in your school using just one succinct sentence or phrase, what would it be? As you consider your response, here are two questions to ponder:

- Are your teachers thriving or merely surviving?
- Are your teachers showing up because they want to or only because they must be present?

Teaching can be a lonely profession, with teachers too often spending much of their time interacting with students and having little opportunity to meet with their peers. And all too often, conversations between teachers and leaders unfold on an ad hoc basis, when a situation requires administrative oversight. Patterns of conversation might also affect teacher efficacy, leading to larger issues in the schoolhouse. Teachers who leave the profession tend to talk about the lack of support they received from their school leadership. They typically mention that they wanted to feel that school leaders cared about them, and they wanted support in developing their individual skills as educators. They wanted to be seen, heard, pushed, and celebrated. C.R.A.F.T. conversations allow you to do all these things and more.

Starting from Day One

School culture evolves in an environment that invites and welcomes its members and is something that has to be attended to daily. But school leaders can use some specific methods from the first day of preplanning to develop a culture in which C.R.A.F.T. conversations are the norm. As you think about creating a culture of belonging, consider the following questions:

- What are the things you currently do to kick off your school year?
- Do you set a theme?
- Do you have a fun faculty gathering?

If you are trying to embed C.R.A.F.T. conversations in your school culture, set the tone from the very beginning. Launching the school year with a staff meeting, a motivational speaker, or a catered lunch are common ways to do this. Another is something we call a C.R.A.F.T. Conversation Café.

A C.R.A.F.T. Conversation Café is a great way to introduce key elements of C.R.A.F.T. conversations to your staff and to start garnering buy-in immediately. We have established the following protocol to give you an organized and efficient way to start laying the foundation for C.R.A.F.T. conversations. You can use this protocol at the beginning of the year or at the beginning of a semester.

C.R.A.F.T. Conversation Café Protocol

- **Time of year:** Preplanning period, summer staff retreat, or midyear reboot
- **Materials:** Five large sheets of butcher/bulletin board paper, large supply of sticky notes, markers, pens/pencils, timer
- **Location:** A large space such as a cafeteria, gym, or media center
- **Time:** 1 1/2 hours (minimum)
- **Set-up:** Post a sheet of butcher paper in each of five different areas. Each section will have one of the letters and the associated word for the acronym *C.R.A.F.T.*
- **Grouping:** Divide staff into five equal-size groups by having participants number off. Each participant should have a supply of sticky notes (so thoughts can be grouped and moved easily) and something to write with.

Opening instructions: "Today we will be C.R.A.F.T.ing our Statements of Commitment for the year as a team. Think about how being *clear, realistic, appropriate, flexible,* and *timely* can shape our conversations throughout the year. You have been divided into five groups. Portions of this activity are designed to be done through silent reflection. The last round involves collaborative thought. Please respect the silence of your thought partners during the silent periods. Feel free to chat during transitions from one station to another."

Round 1: Set a timer to sound every 3 minutes, for a total of 15 minutes, as a signal for groups to move to the next station.

Round 1 instructions to read: "During this first round of rotations, each of you should write statements on your sticky notes using the word at each station to express a commitment for the school year. Write as many sentences as you can during each 3-minute period. Use a new sticky note for each thought and stick it on the butcher paper as you finish each sentence or statement. Are there any questions? Begin at your first station."

[Time the groups for 3-minute rounds. After each group has rotated through each station, read the instructions for the next round.]

Round 2 instructions to read: "For Round 2 rotations, you will begin at the letter you started with. You will have two timed segments at each letter during this round. During the first 3 minutes, you will silently read the statements on the sticky notes. During the next 3 minutes, you will work with your thought partners to arrange the statements into common themes. Are there any questions? Rotate and begin silently reading all of the comments posted."

After 3 minutes have elapsed, read: "For the next 3 minutes, stay at your station and work as a team to group the statements into common themes. Are there any questions? Begin grouping."

Once groups have moved to their second station, read: "For the remaining four stations, you will silently read the statements that have been grouped. After reading the grouped statements silently for 3 minutes, you will work with your thought partners to see if you agree with the groupings or if anything needs to be rearranged, regrouped, or combined. Are there any questions? You may begin your silent reading of the grouped comments."

Here are a few cues to support the facilitation of this protocol. The facilitator could engage the group in rearranging comments, eliminating duplicate comments, or adding additional thoughts that come to mind in the reflective rotations.

[Continue until all groups have cycled through the remaining stations.]

Final round: The final round is when the group members address one of the letters and come up with an agreed-upon standard operating procedure for the year, incorporating their assigned word in a concise statement.

Instructions to read for the final round: "Your group will now rotate back to the station where you started. You will take no more than 5 minutes to develop one concise statement using your word—either *clear, realistic, appropriate, flexible,* or *timely*—to define how we as a school will incorporate these basic C.R.A.F.T. principles into our daily practice this school year. Remove all the sticky notes from the chart paper and write the statement big enough for the other groups to see. Are there any questions? You may begin."

Closing activity: Each group reads its finalized statement and offers a brief explanation. Begin the rotation with *C* and then move on to the other letters.

Debrief: In established collaborative groups (grade levels or subjects taught), have teachers review the agreed-upon C.R.A.F.T. statements and discuss how they will incorporate them into their day-to-day activities and collaborative planning sessions.

Instructions to read for debrief: "Next, you will move to your grade-level teams [use groups established in your school]. With this group, review all five C.R.A.F.T. statements and decide how you will incorporate them into your day-to-day practice and weekly collaborative meetings. One member of your team should attach a post to the discussion board set up in our online forum. Are there any questions? Once your group posting is submitted, you are released to go back to your classroom."

Follow-up: Print posters with statements to post throughout the building and in teacher classrooms. Develop a team planning tool to use for meeting minutes that includes the agreed-upon C.R.A.F.T. statements.

By engaging in a C.R.A.F.T. Conversation Café, you are laying the foundation for C.R.A.F.T. conversations and are allowing teachers to reflect on some of the most important aspects of these types of exchanges. Although your teachers will not walk away understanding every component of a C.R.A.F.T. conversation, they will leave with a tangible understanding of a few of its guiding principles and, we hope, wanting to know more. Remember, this is not a "one time and forget it" scenario. If you complete the follow-up activities suggested and incorporate some of the teacher-generated ideas from the debrief sessions throughout the school year, you can ensure that you are continuously circling back to the basics of C.R.A.F.T. conversations.

Partnerships Paired with C.R.A.F.T. Conversations

As you begin to shift over to C.R.A.F.T. conversations as part of the way of life at your school, it is important to remember that you should not take this step alone. If you are the only one in your building operating with the C.R.A.F.T. mindset, then you will be limited in your progress. It is crucial to consider the other stakeholders in your building and take them along on your journey. We use the word *stakeholder* to urge you to not limit your scope to other administrators and established leaders in your building. As leaders, we tend to overuse the same individuals and not take the opportunity to discover and cultivate new talent. As you work through your C.R.A.F.T. Conversation Café protocol and begin to use C.R.A.F.T. conversations in your school, new faces will emerge. Partner with those individuals who see the value of

C.R.A.F.T. conversations early on and are eager to grow individually and collectively.

Some staff members might need more information before taking the plunge. That's OK too! There is no need to make the other components of C.R.A.F.T. conversations, such as the four cornerstones, a secret. Why not use this book for a yearlong book study? In doing so, you are providing your teachers with a learning experience that is interactive and allowing them to collectively reflect on the value of C.R.A.F.T. conversations and how they can be used within the school community. A book study will also be a valuable exercise for you as a leader, as teachers will undoubtedly have questions about what they read. You will have an opportunity to test your own knowledge of C.R.A.F.T. conversations and to further understand how they can best support your teachers. The book-study approach can enlist participation from all subsets of your building and will provide an easy reference for you to use throughout the year. By reading this book as a team, you are setting clear expectations for your staff and simultaneously setting yourself up for even greater levels of success.

Remember the ripple effect discussed in Chapter 6? The lasting impact that C.R.A.F.T. conversations can have starts with you as the building leader; then it spreads to influence teachers, and finally it extends to students and the larger school community. Just imagine how powerful the ripple effect can be if other leaders and teachers place themselves at the center! The only way for this to occur is by continually building new collaborative partnerships across the different groups already established in your building. Think *joint responsibility*. If you are truly committed to the success of your school, partnerships will make all the difference, enabling C.R.A.F.T. conversations to take place even when you are not in the room.

Rooting C.R.A.F.T. Conversations in the Four Cornerstones

In Chapter 2 we introduced the four cornerstones of C.R.A.F.T. conversations: Building Capacity, Invoking Change, Promoting Collaboration, and Prioritizing Celebration. Figure 2.1 (p. 27) provided you with a visual of the embedded nature of the cornerstones, with building capacity at the heart of it all. This configuration was intentional, as building capacity should be at the center of all that you do as a school leader. Whether your school is a blue-ribbon, award-winning institution or is facing the challenge of keeping its accreditation, it is the leader's job to grow teachers by meeting them where they are and building them up. If your teachers aren't learning, it is unlikely that students' potential to learn is increasing.

A focus on building capacity makes achieving the other cornerstones easier. For example, let's say you notice a trend in your 6th grade math classrooms showing that students are unable to use grade-level math vocabulary to engage in robust discussions. You might be tempted to hinge your C.R.A.F.T. conversation on the Invoking Change cornerstone. After all, you want to see a change! However, your early conversations should focus on the cornerstone of Building Capacity, addressing questions such as "Why is math vocabulary important?" and "What are some innovative ways to introduce vocabulary and encourage its use in the classroom setting?" Once you are confident that teachers agree on why math vocabulary is important and ways in which they can encourage its use daily, then you are ready to focus on supporting them in modifying their current practices.

Although building capacity is of the essence, the other cornerstones are equally valuable when building or sustaining a successful school. It is important to think about each one of your C.R.A.F.T. conversations as an opportunity to engage in at least one of the cornerstones—if not more. Leaders often pigeonhole a C.R.A.F.T. conversation, telling themselves that it is capable of doing only one thing at a time. This limiting viewpoint takes away from the power of C.R.A.F.T. conversations.

When you prepare for a C.R.A.F.T. conversation, determine which cornerstone will be your primary area of focus and why. If you are having difficulty identifying a cornerstone to focus on, go back to the purpose of your conversation. The purpose should directly align to a specific cornerstone. Once you have selected the cornerstone that your conversation will center on, ask yourself whether another cornerstone can be included. Do not force it! The process of focusing on multiple cornerstones should occur naturally.

Perhaps you are having a conversation with your content leads about best practices you have observed in each department. You have artifacts to support the conclusion that many of these key practices have led to increased student achievement, and you would like to see a few of them incorporated across all content areas. Although the cornerstone of Invoking Change might be at the heart of this C.R.A.F.T. conversation, you can see how the Promoting Collaboration cornerstone can be embedded not only in the conversation itself, but also through reflection and follow-up. The point is, don't always begin with the Invoking Change cornerstone. Examine the other three cornerstones as well, and see if you can include all four in a conversation.

In many cases, leaders think of the four cornerstones only when planning and engaging in their C.R.A.F.T. conversations. It is easy to forget how valuable the cornerstones can be when reflecting and following up on an ongoing basis. As you reflect continuously on your conversations and the work of your teachers, you should be engaging in follow-up activities that bring the cornerstones to life. Ask yourself questions such as "Does this activity promote collaboration?" or "In what ways will these touchpoints help build the capacity of the teacher?" Follow-up activities should always directly align with your chosen cornerstones.

Ongoing reflection as it pertains to the cornerstones can also provide leaders with helpful data on their school to help set future goals. It is not necessary to keep a tally of how many C.R.A.F.T. conversations fall under each cornerstone, but as the school year progresses, it will become obvious which cornerstones occupy most of your time. As discussed earlier, you might find that most of your C.R.A.F.T. conversations center on building capacity. However, what if your reflections reveal that prioritizing celebration has never been a focal point? This type of data can reveal truths about the current status of your school and your leadership style.

All C.R.A.F.T. conversations should be rooted in at least one cornerstone. The key is to be intentional and to let the purpose of each C.R.A.F.T. conversation steer you in the right direction. Think about the cornerstone questions that appear throughout the book as additional supports to help guide your thoughts and reflections and solidify your cornerstone selection. Although the cornerstone of Building Capacity will be a focal point for most school leaders, there will be many opportunities to use C.R.A.F.T. conversations to address the cornerstones of Invoking Change, Promoting Collaboration, and Prioritizing Celebration as well. The cornerstones are essential as you plan and execute C.R.A.F.T. conversations, but they are also critical once the conversation has ended. Cornerstones should be used during reflection and follow-up to help you maintain focus on specific goals and better understand your school climate and culture.

Setting C.R.A.F.T. Conversations Apart

When you visualize having C.R.A.F.T. conversations in your school, you can probably see yourself sitting across from one of your teachers. You see the moving of lips, the nodding of heads, the jotting of notes, and maybe even a few high-fives if you're lucky. Leaders tend to visualize the engagement component of the conversation because it centers on dialogue and discussion. However, C.R.A.F.T. conversations recognize that dialogue is only one piece of the puzzle.

C.R.A.F.T. conversations cannot be successful without proper planning. Planning is involved in almost every aspect of a C.R.A.F.T. conversation, from figuring out how to get to know your teachers to determining how and when you will reflect. It is no secret that effective planning takes time and attention to detail. Knowing this is half the battle. Set yourself up for success by scheduling your time wisely and making planning a priority during the week.

We also advise that you determine methods of planning that work best for you based on the different components of a C.R.A.F.T. conversation. For example, when planning for the engagement component, you might find it useful to write down a few potential questions, ensuring that they are open-ended (remember the importance of *not* using closed or leading questions). When planning for your follow-up activities, it might be beneficial to set aside some time to meet with instructional coaches or other teacher leaders in your building. Over time, you will find yourself gravitating to certain methods. Find what works and stick to it.

It is easy to focus on the opening and engaging components of a C.R.A.F.T. conversation. You might start out by thinking about where you will meet with the teacher, or perhaps you need to fine-tune the purpose of the conversation or identify artifacts that will guide the conversation. All these details are important and deserve your attention. However, the closing is equally important. The closing is often forgotten or excluded due to time constraints. If you do not plan to spend time closing your conversation with the same intention and focus that you started with, you might as well not even have the conversation.

Teachers deserve a proper closing to each C.R.A.F.T. conversation that clearly outlines the supports they will receive and the ways in which they can measure their own success. The closing is also an opportunity for you to answer any lingering questions and make sure the teacher feels like he or she has the tools to take immediate action. Although you should take time to summarize the conversation, do not look at the closing as a quick review of a giant to-do list. The closing should be positive and encouraging. Without an effective closing, you will lose most, if not all, of the momentum built up during the conversation. If you want to give teachers a head start toward the goal, close the C.R.A.F.T. conversation with care.

Reflection and follow-up are the last two components of a C.R.A.F.T. conversation. Part of what makes these components unique is that they both occur after the conversation has ended. That is why it is critical to remember that both components must be ongoing. Reflecting only immediately after the conversation is over or planning follow-up activities with no room for flexibility makes it impossible to truly work collaboratively with teachers throughout their professional journey.

When you engage in ongoing reflection and ongoing follow-up, you are constantly checking in with the teacher, with yourself, and with other leaders in your building. Ongoing reflection gives you the time and space to think about what is working and what is not. It allows you to draw on your own observations and expertise as well as that of your team to change course when needed to best support the teacher. Ongoing follow-up works in a similar way by providing you with opportunities to measure success and further address individual teachers' unique needs. When you reflect and follow up consistently, you are able to identify praiseworthy activity, confront any challenges in a timely manner, and redesign supports to meet teachers where they are every step of the way.

Closing Thoughts

As a school leader, your goal is to improve student achievement. It is not possible to improve student achievement without investing in your teachers each and every day. Connecting with your teachers through honest and open dialogue fosters an environment where teachers want to stay and where they feel empowered to change their practice in ways both big and small. This is the essence of what C.R.A.F.T. conversations can do.

If you were not interested in using conversations as a vehicle toward school improvement, this book would likely still be sitting on the shelf. We hope that reading this book has given you a solid understanding of what C.R.A.F.T. conversations are and exactly how they can be used in your school. So the question is, are you ready? Yes! You have the tools, and now it is up to you to use them. You will face some challenges and hit a few bumps in the road, but you will also find that once the power of C.R.A.F.T. conversations is unleashed, it is unstoppable.

References

Agno, J. G. (2010, February 4). What is leadership? [Blog post]. *Coaching Tip: The Leadership Blog.* Retrieved from https://coachingtip.blogs.com/what_can_it_be/2010/02/what-is-leadership.html

ASCD. (2018). School culture and climate. Topics. Retrieved from http://www.ascd.org/research-a-topic/school-culture-and-climate-resources.aspx

Brett, R. (n.d.). Retrieved from https://www.brainyquote.com/quotes/regina_brett_586799

Burkhauser, S. (2017). How much do school principals matter when it comes to teacher working conditions? *Educational Evaluation and Policy Analysis, 39*(1), 126–145.

Bustamante, R. M., Nelson, J. A., & Onwuegbuzie, A. J. (2009). Assessing schoolwide cultural competence: Implications for school leadership preparation. *Educational Administration Quarterly, 45*(5), 793–827.

Cicero, M. T. (n.d.). Retrieved from https://www.brainyquote.com/quotes/marcus_tullius_cicero_379106

Clifford, M., Menon, R., Gangi, T., Condon, C., & Hornung, K. (2012). *Measuring school climate for gauging principal performance: A review of the validity and reliability of publicly accessible measures* (Quality School Leadership Issue Brief). Retrieved from https://www.air.org/sites/default/files/downloads/report/school_climate2_0.pdf

Craddick, C. (2017, May 3). How your body language impacts workplace conversations [Blog post]. *Fierce.* Retrieved from https://fierceinc.com/blog/how-your-body-language-impacts-workplace-conversations

Drago-Severson, E. (2012). New opportunities for principal leadership: Shaping school climates for enhanced teacher development. *Teachers College Record, 114*(3), 1–44. Retrieved from http://www.tcrecord.org/Content.asp?ContentId=16304

Kadem Education, LLC. (2019). Cultural drivers and descriptions. Retrieved from https://kademeducation.com/

Knight, J. (2011). *Unmistakable impact: A partnership approach for dramatically improving instruction.* Thousand Oaks, CA: Corwin.

Knight, J. (2017, June 26). *Should coaching be confidential?* [Video]. Instructional Coaching Group. Retrieved from https://www.instructionalcoaching.com/should-coaching-be-confidential/

Kraft, M. A., Marinell, W. H., & Shen-Wei Yee, D. (2016). School organizational contexts, teacher turnover, and student achievement: Evidence from panel data. *American Educational Research Journal, 53*(5), 1411–1449.

Lemov, D. (2010). *Teach like a champion: 49 techniques that put students on the path to college.* San Francisco: John Wiley & Sons.

Lofthouse, R., Leat, D., & Towler, C. (2010). *Coaching for teaching and learning: A practical guide for schools.* Reading, Berkshire, UK: CfBT Education Trust. Retrieved from https://www.ncl.ac.uk/media/wwwnclacuk/cflat/files/coaching-for-teaching.pdf

Lunenburg, F. C. (2010). Louder than words: The hidden power of nonverbal communication in the workplace. *International Journal of Scholarly Academic Intellectual Diversity, 12*(1), 1–5. Retrieved from http://www.nationalforum.com/Electronic%20Journal%20Volumes/Lunenburg,%20Fred%20C%20Louder%20Than%20Words%20IJSAID%20V12%20N1%202010.pdf

Marshall, J. (n.d.). Retrieved from https://allauthor.com/quotes/author/john-marshall/?topic=communication

Maye, R. (n.d.). Retrieved from https://mostphrases.blogspot.com/2017/08/conversation-sayings-and-quotes.html

Mehrabian, A. (1971). *Silent messages.* Belmont, CA: Wadsworth.

Saphier, J., & King, M. (1985, March). Good seeds grow in strong cultures. *Educational Leadership, 42*(6), 67–74. Retrieved from http://www.ascd.org/ASCD/pdf/journals/ed_lead/el_198503_saphier.pdf

Wheatley, M. J. (2002). *Turning to one another: Simple conversations to restore hope to the future.* San Francisco: Berrett-Koehler.

Yesbeck, D. M. (2015). School climate: Hot or cold? *International Journal of Education and Social Science, 2*(6), 1–4. Retrieved from http://www.ijessnet.com/wp-content/uploads/2015/07/1.pdf

Zeldin, T. (1998). *Conversation: How talk can change our lives.* Santa Monica, CA: Hidden Spring.

Zepeda, S. J. (2015). *Job-embedded professional development: Support, collaboration, and learning in schools.* New York: Routledge.

Zepeda, S. J. (2017). *Instructional supervision: Applying tools and concepts* (4th ed.). New York: Routledge.

Suggested Readings

Abrahams, J. (2016). *Hard conversations unpacked: The whos, the whens, and the what-ifs.* Thousand Oaks, CA: Corwin.

Baeder, J. (2018). *Now we're talking! 21 days to high-performance instructional leadership.* Bloomington, IN: Solution Tree Press.

Caposey, PJ. (2018). *Manage your time or time will manage you: Strategies that work from an educator who has been there.* Alexandria, VA: ASCD.

DeWitt, P. M. (2019). *Coach it further: Using the art of coaching to improve school leadership.* Thousand Oaks, CA: Corwin.

Drago-Severson, E., & Blum-DeStefano, J. (2018). *Leading change together: Developing educator capacity within schools and systems.* Alexandria, VA: ASCD.

Gross Cheliotes, L. M., & Reilly, M. F. (2018). *Coaching conversations: Transforming your school one conversation at a time* (2nd ed.). Thousand Oaks, CA: Corwin.

Gruenert, S., & Whitaker, T. (2017). *School culture recharged: Strategies to energize your staff and culture.* Alexandria, VA: ASCD.

Hayashi, S. K. (2010). *Conversations for change: 12 ways to say it right when it matters most.* New York: McGraw-Hill.

Johnson, J., Leibowitz, S., & Perret, K. (2017). *The coach approach to school leadership: Leading teachers to higher levels of effectiveness.* Alexandria, VA: ASCD.

Jones, J., & Vari, T. J. (2018). *Candid and compassionate feedback: Transforming everyday practices in schools.* New York: Routledge.

Jung, L. A. (2017). How to keep mutiny from sinking your change effort. *Educational Leadership, 74*(1), 28–32. Retrieved from http://www.ascd.org/publications/educational-leadership/jun17/vol74/num09/How-to-Keep-Mutiny-from-Sinking-Your-Change-Effort.aspx

Knight, J. (2016). *Better conversations: Coaching ourselves and each other to be more credible, caring, and connected.* Thousand Oaks, CA: Corwin.

Muhammad, A. (2018). *Transforming school culture: How to overcome staff division* (2nd ed.). Bloomington, IN: Solution Tree.

Novick, B. (2015). Ten tips for tackling tough conversations. *Educational Leadership, 72*(7), 80–81. Retrieved from http://www.ascd.org/publications/educational-leadership/apr15/vol72/num07/Ten-Tips-for-Tackling-Tough-Conversations.aspx

Ronfeldt, M., Farmer, S. O., McQueen, K., & Grissom, J. A. (2015). Teacher collaboration in instructional teams and student achievement. *American Educational Research Journal, 52*(3), 475–514. doi:10.3102/0002831215585562

Rushton, R. (2018). *The power of connection: How to become a master communicator in your workplace, your head space and at your place.* Hoboken, NJ: John Wiley and Sons.

Smith, R., & Campbell, M. (2011). *Talent conversations: What they are, why they're crucial and how to do them right.* Greensboro, NC: Center for Creative Leadership.

Thompson, G. (2017). *The master coach: Leading with character, building connections, and engaging in extraordinary conversations.* New York: Select Books.

Venables, D. R. (2017). *Facilitating teacher teams and authentic PLCs: The human side of leading people, protocols, and practices.* Alexandria, VA: ASCD.

Whitaker, T., Zoul, J., & Casas, J. (2015). *What connected educators do differently.* New York: Routledge.

Zepeda, S. J. (Ed.). (2018). *The job-embedded nature of coaching: Lessons and insights for school leaders at all levels.* Lanham, MD: Rowman & Littlefield.

Index

Note: Page references followed by an italicized *f* indicate information contained in figures.

About the Authors

Sally J. Zepeda, PhD, is a professor in the Department of Lifelong Education, Administration, and Policy at the University of Georgia. Her research and service focus on instructional supervision, teacher and leader evaluation, and professional development for preK–12 educators. Her scholarship has appeared in journals such as the *Review of Educational Research*, the *Journal of School Leadership*, the *Alberta Journal of Educational Research,* and *Educational Leadership*. Now in its fourth edition, her text *Instructional Supervision: Applying Tools and Concepts* was translated into Turkish. She has worked with numerous school systems in the United States and the Middle East to develop coaching and mentoring programs for teachers and leaders.

Lakesha Robinson Goff, EdD, has served as a teacher of mathematics at some of the nation's most unique and innovative schools, such as the SEED Public Charter School in Washington, D.C., and the Ron Clark Academy in Atlanta, Georgia. She has served as an assistant principal at Ivy Preparatory Young Men's Leadership Academy in Atlanta and at Centennial Academy in Atlanta Public Schools and as a manager of teacher leadership development with Teach for America (Metro Atlanta). Her extensive experience in providing large-scale professional development and in coaching educators includes serving as a guest facilitator at the Oprah Winfrey Leadership Academy for Girls in South Africa.

Stefanie W. Steele, PhD, earned her terminal degree in educational administration and policy from the University of Georgia, where she also received her Bachelor of Science degree and Master of Education degree. Since 2002, she has been an assistant principal at the middle and high school levels in the Gwinnett County Public School District, a metro-Atlanta school system. She has served in leadership roles for special education, technology, professional learning, curriculum, and assessment, and she has taught courses in professional learning at the University of Georgia.

Related ASCD Resources

At the time of publication, the following resources were available (ASCD stock numbers appear in parentheses).

Print Products

100+ Ways to Recognize and Reward Your School Staff by Emily E. Houck (#112051)

The Coach Approach to School Leadership: Leading Teachers to Higher Levels of Effectiveness by Jessica Johnson, Shira Leibowitz, and Kathy Perret (#117025)

Committing to the Culture: How Leaders Can Create and Sustain Positive Schools by Steve Gruenert and Todd Whitaker (#119007)

Creating a Culture of Reflective Practice: Capacity Building for Schoolwide Success by Pete Hall and Alisa Simeral (#117006)

Design Thinking for School Leaders: Five Roles and Mindsets That Ignite Positive Change by Alyssa Gallagher and Kami Thordarson (#118022)

Leading Change Together: Developing Educator Capacity Within Schools and Systems by Eleanor Drago-Severson and Jessica Blum-DeStefano (#117027)

Navigating the Principalship: Key Insights for New and Aspiring School Leaders by James P. Spillane and Rebecca Lowenhaupt (#118017)

Never Underestimate Your Teachers: Instructional Leadership for Excellence in Every Classroom by Robyn R. Jackson (#110028)

For up-to-date information about ASCD resources, go to www.ascd.org. You can search the complete archives of Educational Leadership at www.ascd.org/el.

DVD

The Reflective Educator: A Collaborative Approach to Building Teachers' Capacity DVD by Peter A. Hall and Alisa Simeral (#616027)

PD Online

Building Teachers' Capacity for Success: Instructional Coaching Essentials by Peter A. Hall and Alisa Simeral (#PD15OC005S)

FIT Teaching in Action for Instructional Leaders by Nancy E. Frey, Stefani Hite, and Douglas B. Fisher (#PD17OC002M)

Leading Professional Learning: Building Capacity Through Teacher Leaders by Judy F. Carr (#PD13OC010S)

ASCD myTeachSource®

Download resources from a professional learning platform with hundreds of research-based best practices and tools for your classroom at http://myteach source.ascd.org/.

For more information, send an e-mail to member@ascd.org; call 1-800-933-2723 or 703-578-9600; send a fax to 703-575-5400; or write to Information Services, ASCD, 1703 N. Beauregard St., Alexandria, VA 22311-1714 USA.

THE WHOLE CHILD

The ASCD Whole Child approach is an effort to transition from a focus on narrowly defined academic achievement to one that promotes the long-term development and success of all children. Through this approach, ASCD supports educators, families, community members, and policymakers as they move from a vision about educating the whole child to sustainable, collaborative actions.

C.R.A.F.T. Conversations for Teacher Growth relates to the **engaged, supported,** and **challenged** tenets.

For more about the ASCD Whole Child approach, visit **www.ascd.org/wholechild.**

WHOLE CHILD
TENETS

1 HEALTHY
Each student enters school healthy and learns about and practices a healthy lifestyle.

2 SAFE
Each student learns in an environment that is physically and emotionally safe for students and adults.

3 ENGAGED
Each student is actively engaged in learning and is connected to the school and broader community.

4 SUPPORTED
Each student has access to personalized learning and is supported by qualified, caring adults.

5 CHALLENGED
Each student is challenged academically and prepared for success in college or further study and for employment and participation in a global environment.

LEARN. TEACH. LEAD.